# CULTURES OF THE WORLD®

# POLAND

### Jay Heale & Paweł Grajnert

**BENCHMARK BOOKS**

MARSHALL CAVENDISH
NEW YORK

**PICTURE CREDITS**

Cover photo: © Getty Images: The Image Bank/Angelo Cavalli
age fotostock: 113 • alt.TYPE/REUTERS: 35, 88, 114 • ANA Press Agency: 50, 54, 96, 108 • Corbis Inc.:
40, 51 • Getty Images: 30, 130 • HBL Network Photo Agency: 6, 122 • Jay Heale: 10, 41, 72, 80, 89, 100,
107, 124 • Hulton-Deutsch Collection: 28, 81 • Hutchison Library: 13, 20, 27, 66, 86 • Image Bank: 23,
24, 43, 56, 58 • Life File Photo Library: 3, 7, 8, 15, 16, 29, 33, 36, 37, 38, 39, 45, 60, 65, 67, 70, 71, 73, 74,
75, 83, 85, 91, 92, 93, 94, 97, 98, 105, 106, 112, 118, 120, 123, 128 • Lonely Planet Images: 18 • Yiorgos
Nikiteas/Eye Ubiquitous: 48 • Polska Agencja Informacyjna Redakcja Fotografii i Wystaw: 14, 17, 32, 61,
68, 99, 110, 115, 117, 129 • STOCKFOOD/HRBKOVA A.: 131 • Sylvia Cordaiy Photo Library: 5, 12, 42, 62
• Tan Chung Lee: 4, 9, 52, 59, 63, 64, 69, 75, 76, 79, 102, 126 • TopFoto: 84 • Travel Ink Ltd: 46 • Anna
Tully/Hutchison Library: 1 • Philip Wolmuth/Hutchison Library: 78

**ACKNOWLEDGMENTS**

Thanks to Christopher Howard of Indiana University for his expert reading of this manuscript.

**PRECEDING PAGE**

Polish children in traditional dress perform at a folk dance festival.

Marshall Cavendish Benchmark
99 White Plains Road
Tarrytown, NY 10591
Website: www.marshallcavendish.us

Originated and designed by Times Editions
An imprint of Marshall Cavendish International (Asia) Private Limited
A member of Times Publishing Limited

*Library of Congress Cataloging-in-Publication Data*
Heale, Jay.
   Poland / by Jay Heale.
      p. cm. — (Cultures of the world)
   Summary: "Explores the geography, history, government, economy, people, and culture of Poland"
      —Provided by publisher.
   Includes bibliographical references and index.
   ISBN 0-7614-1847-4
   1. Poland—Juvenile literature. I. Title. II. Series: Cultures of the world (2nd ed.).
   DK4147.H4 2005
   943.8—dc22                                     2004027455

Printed in China

7 6 5 4 3 2 1

J914.38
2005

# CONTENTS

A logger in the Tatra Mountains in southern Poland.

Daisies and other wild-flowers cover the mountains and meadows in spring.

# INTRODUCTION

LOCATED IN NORTH-CENTRAL EUROPE, Poland is a country in transition. A newly independent nation, the Polish people are enjoying the results of a centuries-old struggle for democracy and self-determination that began under Poland's first leader, Mieszko I, in A.D. 966.

As a new member of the European Union, Poland is building its young democracy on a heritage that includes some of the most glorious and infamous achievements in human history. This is a country deeply influenced by clear links to Russia, Germany, Italy, France, Turkey, and Lithuania, among others. But Poland is also a place where the native Slavs fought from generation to generation against numerous foes to retain their identity and liberty.

Poles cherish their freedom. They are a resilient, outspoken people with an ironic sense of humor. "Two Poles, three opinions," says a Polish proverb. "Poland shall not perish as long as we live," says the Polish national anthem.

# GEOGRAPHY

POLAND'S MOUNTAINS AND LAKES are the country's most dramatic features, although the heart of the country is in its spreading plains, dominated by green miles of woods, parks, and small strip-field farms. Elsewhere are grey zones of apartment blocks, houses of unplastered concrete bricks, and industrial works.

Poland is a squarish area of land that stretches from the Baltic Sea in the north to the Carpathian Mountains in the south. Poland's neighbors are: Germany to the west; the Czech Republic and Slovakia to the south; Ukraine and Belarus to the east; and Lithuania and Russia to the northeast. With a total area of 120,728 square miles (312,684 square km), Poland is the ninth largest country in Europe.

Most of Poland is part of the northern European plain. More than 75 percent of the land is less than 650 feet (198 m) above sea level. Poland's largest rivers, the Vistula and the Oder, originate in the Car-

*Above:* **Farmlands color the Polish countryside green.**

*Opposite:* **A change in the Polish seasons turns the greens, reds, and golds of the fall into the white of winter.**

pathian Mountains and wind north across the plains to the Baltic Sea. The central and northern areas are rather sandy and infertile. About 60 percent of the land is farmed, and over a quarter is covered by forests.

The capital of Poland is Warsaw, slightly to the east of the country's geographical center. In the north are the Masurian Lakes; northwest the Baltic coast; southwest the region called Silesia; and south, bordering the Czech Republic and Slovakia, the Tatra and Sudety ranges.

## *SIX CLEAR SEASONS*

Geography books describe Poland's climate as temperate in the west, continental in the east. This is because far to the west is the warm air of the Atlantic Ocean, while to the east cold polar air blows from Russia. Climatic conditions are especially important in Poland, as much of the country depends on local agriculture.

A Polish blizzard, though recent winters have been milder than usual.

Poland has six identifiable seasons. Cold, snowy winter breaks into early spring. Then comes spring, sunny and flower-filled. The short summer, with plenty of rain and sunshine, can be quite hot in the big cities. Summer is followed by the warm, golden fall, with rich colors everywhere. Then, a foggy, humid period heralds the approach of winter. Winter can be bleak in the central plains, so people throng south to the ski slopes of the Tatra Mountain resorts.

The temperature ranges from 76°F (24.4°C) or higher in summer to 20°F (-6.7°C) in the mountains in winter. The record low was -41.1°F (-40.6°C) in 1929, while the record high was 104.4°F (40.2°C) in 1921. The Baltic region is sunniest in summer, while the Carpathian Mountains receive the most sunshine in winter. Annual rainfall ranges from 31 to 47 inches (78.7 to 119.4 cm) in the mountains to 18 inches (45.7 cm) in the middle Polish lowlands, for an annual average of 24 inches (61 cm).

## *A CARPET OF FIELDS*

From the air, much of Poland looks like a carpet of narrow fields and meadows colored with the bright yellow of rape, the warm ocher of wheat and rye, and the fresh green of potato plants—like a patchwork quilt made of thin parallel strips but without any dividing fences.

Before World War I, much of Poland's agricultural land was owned by rich landowners and worked by laborers. When the Communists took power, the government tried to enforce a policy of collective farms. The Poles bitterly resisted the idea of joint ownership and the sharing of proceeds. Only about one-fifth of Polish farmland was collectivized. While young people worked in towns, older people stayed on the farms, so the countryside did not change much. But as Poland integrates into the European Union, modernization and urbanization will displace millions of small farmers, who will not be able to compete with agribusiness.

Freed of their Communist overlords, nearly 3 million Polish farmers own 75 percent of the land. Their largest crop is rye, amounting to some 6.2 million tons, the world's largest rye crop after that of the former Soviet Union. Poland's other crops include wheat, barley, oats, sugar beets, fruit such as blueberries, strawberries, and blackcurrants, and vegetables such as potatoes, cabbages, onions, and beetroot. Oak, pine, and birch trees line country roads. Pine makes up more than half of the forested land. There are also larch and beech, with spruce fir on the mountain slopes.

**Vegetables are grown everywhere in Poland, and market stalls overflow with beets, carrots, and other vegetables.**

## *INDUSTRY*

Poland has extensive mineral deposits. Silesia, in the southwest, has one of the world's largest reserves of bituminous coal. There is sulfur near Tarnobrzeg, zinc and lead near Katowice, and lignite (brown coal), rock salt, natural gas, and copper elsewhere. Wieliczka, 5 miles (8 km) southeast of Krakow, is the oldest salt mine in Europe and has been operating for more than 700 years. It is not surprising then that southwestern Poland is the country's most industrialized area. The Upper Silesian-Moravian coal field is the second largest coal field in Europe, exceeded only by the German Ruhr.

**Residents of the town of Katowice live in close proximity to industrial buildings.**

Since the 1990s, the Polish government has been privatizing or closing inefficient and unprofitable factories and mines. Many of the traditionally high-paying industrial jobs are gone, and more people are now employed in the service sector.

The old royal city of Krakow stands about 40 miles (64 km) east of the main mining area. Wroclaw, on the Oder River, is an important industrial center about 90 miles (144.8 km) to the north-northwest. Lodz is the center of Poland's textile industry. Cottons, woolens, silks, and linens are made there. Poland was, for some time, Europe's largest producer of flax and has a significant linen industry.

## DEVASTATING POLLUTION

Northwest of Krakow is the old industrial center of Katowice, where coal, zinc, lead, and silver have been mined for hundreds of years. Today, large quantities of poor-quality coal are burned to power industry and heat homes, and the air reeks of sulfur. The area is an unsightly urban-industrial sprawl, with huge waste heaps and lakes of polluted water beside coal mines and factories, while rows of grubby houses, schools, and shops fill the gaps between.

The medieval buildings of sandstone and limestone in Krakow are being eaten away by the polluted air. Sulfur levels are 250 percent higher than Polish safety limits, and these are four times higher than those set by the United States. The Katowice region has the highest rate of stillbirths and birth defects in the whole country. Several factories have been closed to reduce the amount of pollution being generated.

In southwestern Poland, among the forests near the border, stands the resort town of Jelenia Gora. The area is affected by acid rain, which officials say comes from across the border. The old forests, once rich with spruce and pine, are now dying. Some blame fluorides washed out of the smoke; others say the soil has turned acid. Whatever the reason, the trees lose more and more needles and eventually die. Where once there were green crowns, now grey trunks remain.

**NOWA HUTA** From the steeples of Krakow, the smoking chimneys of Nowa Huta, or New Mill, can be seen. This was once the Communist idea of "the workers' dream city." Slogans promised high wages, double food rations, modern quarters, medical care, and "a dazzling, unclouded future." Hopeful workers crowded in from the countryside and found themselves housed in huge grey apartment blocks with electric lights, kitchens, and bathrooms. As steel production began, so did pollution, and soon not a tree was to be seen anywhere in the model socialist city.

There was a political motivation behind the building of Nowa Huta so close to a city of historic importance. Krakow was the former royal city of Poland, with one of Europe's oldest universities and a large, educated middle class. The state hoped to change the socioeconomic status by creating lots of blue-collar jobs and thus increasing the number of workers, who according to socialist theories would take the leading role in society. But instead, the intellectuals and workers joined hands: with the advice and guidance of the intellectuals, the workers organized and subsequently posed a real problem for the Communist government.

## WARSAW

Stories say that the greatest river in Poland, the Vistula, once harbored a mermaid. This mythical being is now found on Warsaw's coat of arms.

Sadly, this historic city is now surrounded by seemingly endless grey housing estates. Fortunately, the busy roads lead straight to the more attractive modern city center, built around the landmark Palace of Culture and Science. The more historic parts of Warsaw, as well as the newer residential areas, are on the Vistula's western bank. The eastern bank, the Praga, escaped war damage because the Red Army occupied it before the Nazis were able to level it as they did the rest of Warsaw.

The column of Zygmund III Wasa, the king who moved Poland's royal capital from Krakow to Warsaw in 1596, stands in the center of Castle Square. The statue is Warsaw's oldest monument and was the first to be rebuilt after World War II. In the square, horses clip-clop on the cobblestones, pulling carriages past open-air cafés, artists, souvenir and flower stalls, and camera-toting tourists.

Tourists visit the Royal Castle, with its beautifully restored interior, the Historical Museum, and the Cathedral of Saint John—the scene of some of the most bitter fighting

## A CITY REBUILT

At the end of World War II, Warsaw lay in ruins, a victim of systematic Nazi destruction. In a strangely uncharacteristic mood, the new Communist rulers chose to rebuild old Warsaw rather than replace it with cheap, stark Stalinist housing projects. So, working from old prints and paintings, this historic city was painstakingly reconstructed. Paintings of 18th-century Warsaw, saved from the burning ruins of the former Royal Castle, served as architectural models. Twenty million tons of rubble were removed and turned into building material. One hundred carloads of rubble were removed every day. Women and high-school students helped in the rebuilding.

Today, the warm pastel colors of Warsaw's Old Town (*above*) have been preserved, and the past has not been forgotten. Memorial plaques everywhere describe mass executions of civilians, and bullet holes can be seen in the few original sections of the rebuilt houses.

in the Warsaw Uprising in 1944, when more than 250,000 Polish soldiers and civilians were killed during two months of street fighting with the Nazis. Around 85 percent of the city was destroyed. South of the city is the Wilanow Palace, once the summer residence of Jan III Sobieski, a 17th-century Polish king. Visitors to the palace wear felt slippers, obligatory in all Polish museums, as they view superbly painted walls and ceilings, and admire the formal gardens.

*Opposite:* **The Royal Castle in Warsaw.**

A network of hiking trails links the Tatra villages, waterfalls, and lakes. Climbing guides and a mountain rescue service are provided by the local highlanders, the Gorale.

## *MOUNTAIN RANGES*

Poland's southern boundary is formed by a chain of mountain ranges. Snowcapped for much of the year, the High Tatras are the most famous and most popular. Their alpine-style heights offer outdoor adventure for skiers in winter and for hikers and climbers in summer. Rising beyond 8,100 feet (2,469 m), the High Tatras are part of the Carpathian Mountains that straddle Poland, the Czech Republic, and Slovakia.

Farther east, the Pieniny Mountains are cut by the Dunajec River, and to the southwest stands the Beskidy range, picturesque with spruce and beech forests, the source of the Vistula River, which flows across the Polish plain.

The mountains not only provide recreation but also support the important forestry industry. The foothills of the Tatra Mountains are called Podhale (pod-HA-le)—a sparsely populated area of lush meadows. The main town there is Nowy Targ, known for its market that starts at 3 A.M. every Thursday. Deeper into the Tatra Mountains, past steep valleys and quaint villages carved lovingly from the local timber, stands Zakopane, a little mountain town that attracts visitors from all over Poland. It is also a gathering place for artists.

# KRAKOW

Krakow stands where the Tatra Mountains join the Polish plain. The former capital is home to the country's oldest university, Jagiellonian, founded in 1364. Krakow is a completely preserved medieval city, one of only a few Polish cities to escape the devastation of World War II. It is listed by UNESCO as one of the world's 12 most significant historic sites. Krakow's main market square, Rynek Glowny, is Europe's largest square. Cafés, beer gardens, and restaurants line all sides of the square, which serves as a location for local cultural displays. Flower sellers surround the medieval Cloth Hall, now a covered market full of booths selling folk art and typical Polish souvenirs. In a corner of the square stands the magnificent Church of Our Lady Mary.

Wawel Hill, standing on a bend of the Vistula River, is one of the historical gems of Poland. Here the Royal Castle of Wawel sits high on a hill above the Vistula. Rebuilt at the end of the 16th century, the castle boasts a great courtyard and a crypt where Polish kings lie entombed in massive marble. All but four of Poland's 45 monarchs are buried in the Wawel Royal Cathedral. Long lines of visitors walk through rooms decorated in colored marble and priceless Flemish tapestries. One can see such treasures as a jewel-studded shield captured from the Turks at the battle of Vienna in 1683, a velvet hat with a dove embroidered in pearls (given to Jan III Sobieski by the pope after Vienna was saved), and a dazzling robe embroidered with heraldic suns (a gift to Sobieski by French King Louis XIV).

Legend has it that a dragon (*depicted in the sculpture right*) lived in a cave beneath Wawel Hill. Krak, the mythical founder of Krakow, commissioned the slaying of the terrible beast to save his daughter, who was to be sacrificed to the dragon. A humble shoemaker devised a way to kill the beast by feeding it animal skins stuffed with tar and sulfur. The dragon gobbled them up, was driven into a frenzy of thirst, rushed into the Vistula, and drank until it exploded.

Fishing boats at Sopot. There are good fishing grounds in the Baltic, but fishermen have a hard life.

## BALTIC COAST

Poland has a 430-mile (692-km) coastline on the Baltic Sea. Poland's annual catch of fish is 200,000 tons. There are good fishing grounds in the Baltic for cod and herring, but pollution has killed off some species of fish, such as sturgeon.

In the 17th century, Gdansk was more than twice Warsaw's size. Formerly an independent city-state known as Danzig, Gdansk had a multiethnic, multireligious population consisting mainly of Germans, Dutch, Poles, Kaszubians, and Scandinavians. Gdansk, along with other cities, suffered greatly during World War II. The Russians destroyed 90 percent of Gdansk when they "liberated" the town after the German occupation. Gdansk was the birthplace of the free trade union Solidarity.

Gdansk is linked by urban development to its neighbors Sopot and Gdynia, forming what is known as the Tri-City. The polluted waters of the Vistula enter the sea here, affecting the whole bay of Gdansk.

To the east lie the Masurian Lakes, a popular summer destination for sailing and swimming. The main launching point for canoeists and forest hikers is the town of Olsztyn.

## POLISH WILDLIFE

A land so full of ancient forests, tangled lakes, and high mountains has its fair share of wildlife. Large mammals include wild boar, elk, brown bears, and a few herds of the woodland-dwelling European bison. In the High Tatra Mountains, there are chamois and marmot.

On Poland's eastern border, Bialowieza Forest is a national park of more than 300,000 acres (121,406 hectares). It was once home to one of the world's last wild bison herds, but during World War I, hungry soldiers killed all the bison. In 1929 three pairs of bison were brought to the forest from foreign zoos. About 300 bison now roam freely, along with deer, wildcats, lynx, wolves, and beaver, in one of the last fragments of untouched ancient forest in Europe. Here, spruce trees reach 150 feet (45.7 m), creating a great green cathedral. Numerous national parks and conservation sites, with sightseeing spots, are protected and managed by the state. The Tatra Mountains, where some brown bears still live, were included in 1954.

According to the Committee for the Protection of Eagles in Poland, there are some 350 pairs of eagles that are carefully monitored to ensure that they have absolute quiet when hatching their eggs and looking after their fledglings. The eagle is the national emblem of Poland.

Flowers—scarlet poppies, blue cornflowers, white daisies—grow in hedges and the corners of fields, where ploughs cannot reach. In spring, the mountains blush with alpine flowers. But perhaps the greatest natural beauty of Poland is in the deep forests, especially in the fall, when the low sun slants through yellow birch and golden beech trees.

This herd of bison lives in the Bialowieza National Park, part of the largest forest area of the Central European plain.

17

# HISTORY

SLAVIC TRIBES lived in the Vistula river basin for centuries. In the ninth century A.D., several West Slavic tribes united to form small states. One was ruled by the Piast family, which by the mid-900s had united the region surrounding present-day Poznan. In 966, considered the year of Poland's founding, Piast ruler Mieszko I adopted Christianity. During his rule, tribes speaking similar languages were united.

At that time, local noblemen kept private armies, and the countryside was divided into dukedoms and principalities often in conflict with one another. But by 1109 Poland was strong enough to defend against invasions by Germanic tribes from the west, and a network of castles was built to defend the borders.

By the 14th century, Poland was a united kingdom that stretched from the Baltic Sea to the Black Sea. When it united with Lithuania in the 16th century, Poland was the largest country in Europe.

## INVASIONS

The geographical position of Poland, spread across the northern plains between Europe and Asia, made it an easy path for invaders. The Mongol armies of Genghis Khan left trails of destruction in the 13th century, as the knights of Europe were no match for them. Happily for Christendom, the Mongols did not try to conquer Europe, although they did invade twice that century, burning most Polish cities.

The Teutonic Knights, German Crusaders originally organized for services in the Holy Land to provide charity and care of the sick, eventually grew into a powerful military force and became cruel. In 1308 the Teutonic Knights snatched the lands of Pomerania, cutting Poland off from the Baltic Sea and starting 150 years of warfare with Poland that eventually led to their decline.

*Opposite:* **A 17th-century tiled stove in the Gothic castle in Oporow, central Poland.**

## *FENDING OFF ATTACKS*

In the 16th century, the Kingdom of Poland, combined with the Grand Duchy of Lithuania, was the largest state in Europe. In 1558 Tsar Ivan IV (the Terrible) of Russia invaded Livonia (present-day Latvia and Estonia). Poland-Lithuania intervened, and in 1582 Polish King Stefan Batory defeated the Russians.

But in 1655 the Swedes invaded Poland, and their occupation lasted until 1660. In the following decade, Poland fended off more attacks by the Russians and the Ottoman Turks, loosing territory.

In 1674 Jan III Sobieski was elected king of Poland. He made a pact with Leopold I of Austria, who in 1683 called on Sobieski to save Vienna. Reinforcing the army of Charles V, the duke of Lorraine, Sobieski drove back the invading Turks, becoming the savior of Christian Europe.

Polish greatness declined after Sobieski's death in Warsaw in 1696. Weakened by wars with the Turks, disagreements among the nobles, and quarrels at the election of every king, Poland became prey to the greater powers of Europe.

## POLAND VANISHES

In 1772 came the first of three partitions that would eventually erase Poland from the map. Russia, Austria-Hungary, and Prussia seized large portions of Polish territory. Jolted into action, Poland improved its education system and, encouraged by a wave of fresh political thinking, pushed government reforms. In 1791 Poland adopted a new constitution, becoming only the second country in the world, after the United States, to do so.

The envisaged consolidation of royal power and political reorganization brought fierce opposition from Russia, which sent troops into Poland in 1792. The constitution was abolished in 1793, and a second partition was made between Russia and Prussia.

After an uprising in Warsaw, Krakow, and Wilno (Vilnius), in 1795 Russia, Austria-Hungary, and Prussia claimed the last of Poland, which was already a Russian protectorate. Poland disappeared from the map for more than a century.

## FOREIGN RULE

During the 19th century, Polish lands were under the rule of Imperial Russia or the Prussians. After a failed uprising against Russian rule by Polish nationalists in 1831, Russia abolished Polish self-governance and civil liberties. Uprisings against Russian rule in 1846, 1848, and 1863 led to harsh measures at Russification.

Germanization was the rule in Prussian-controlled areas, but the treatment was not as harsh. After the fall of Imperial Russia in 1917, Germany gained control over Russian-held Polish territory. A provisional Polish government was set up in Paris, and the Germans created a regency council for the Polish "kingdom."

## THE NEW NATION

During World War I, U.S. president Woodrow Wilson declared that restoring a reunited, independent Poland was an incontrovertible aim of the Allies. After the Allied victory, Polish independence was proclaimed on November 11, 1918, by Jozef Pilsudski, the founder of the Polish Legions that fought against Germany. On June 28, 1919, the Treaty of Versailles officially recognized Polish independence, although more fighting was to come. In 1920 Poland's attempt to seize Ukraine led to an attack by Russia's Red Army, which soon moved toward Warsaw. Pilsudski led the Polish army in a successful counterattack. Under the Treaty of Riga, Russia ceded a large part of Ukraine to Poland, whose eastern border was fixed on the Zbrucz River. In 1921 the Second Polish Republic adopted the March Constitution, which declared Poland's sovereignty. However, the years following were plagued by political instability. In 1926 Pilsudski seized power in a military coup and governed until his death in 1935.

## WORLD WAR II

On the false pretext that the Polish state was somehow abusing German nationals in and around the city of Danzig (Gdansk), Poland was the first country to be invaded by the Nazis. World War II began at 4:45 A.M. on September 1, 1939, when the German naval vessel *Schleswig-Holstein* bombarded the Polish defensive positions on Westerplatte, an ammunition depot just outside Gdansk. Almost simultaneously, German armored divisions crossed the border into Poland from the west. On September 17, the Red Army invaded in the east. Polish forces fought until September 27, when Warsaw fell. Military aid promised by France and Great Britain never arrived. After a fierce 36-day campaign, Poland was once again divided between Germany and Russia.

## THE "FINAL SOLUTION"

The camps the Nazis built at Majdanek, Treblinka, and Auschwitz-Birkenau were for the specific purpose of destroying a nation. Hitler's "final solution" turned Poland into a mass graveyard.

Auschwitz (*right*), previously a Polish military barracks, became a labor camp for Poles who were considered anti-Nazi. The cynical motto over the gate read *"Arbeit Macht Frei"* ("Work Makes You Free"). Auschwitz was later turned into a station for Jews on their way to the death camp in Birkenau. Today this horrifying site serves as a museum. On display are piles of personal belongings looted from Jewish families before they were murdered. In the barracks, there is a mountain of human hair, with some material woven from it; there are also empty canisters that once contained Zyklon-B (Cyclone B), the hydrogen cyanide compound used to kill inmates.

Block 10 housed the women who were used as subjects in sterilization experiments. Block 11 was the prison within a prison. Inmates accused of serious offences were dumped in tiny damp basement cells, too small to sit or even squat in. Political prisoners were tried and executed.

Birkenau (Auschwitz II) was built as a factory devoted to death. The gas chambers were disguised as huge shower rooms, where more than a million—probably far more—Polish Jews were massacred. Their bodies were at first buried but later burned. Crematoria were constructed to incinerate more than 4,000 bodies in 24 hours. Toward the end of the war, the Nazis destroyed much of Birkenau to keep its grim secrets from being discovered.

Then began a reign of terror, as Hitler wanted racial purity in his widening empire and regarded Poles as subhuman. Those considered at odds with German policy were put into concentration camps, which became death camps. Russia depopulated its share of Poland by deporting between 1 and 2 million Poles in cattle trucks to Siberia and other Russian territories. An underground organization called the Home Army, which consisted of more than 300,000 people, destroyed German communications, blew up bridges, and hindered production of war materials through the entire occupation. In Paris, a Polish government -in-exile was formed in 1939. It later moved to London.

The Unknown Soldier's Tomb lies in Warsaw, a symbol of the thousands who died fighting for their country in World War II.

## A COMMUNIST STATE

When Germany fell on May 8, 1945, Poland had lost around 6 million citizens (according to estimates), the capital was obliterated, and survivors were impoverished. Poland's borders were redrawn, and the country became a Communist state. The party wielded all the power in the new "people's republic," and Communist policy stated that "the land now belongs to the peasants."

Almost every major city except Krakow had to be rebuilt, but in Communist ideology, top priority was given to the building of steel, coal, iron, and armaments industries. Poland joined the Warsaw Pact, the Communist alliance. Daily life became a nightmare under the Soviet regime. Children were encouraged to inform on their parents. People suspected of being hostile to the state were denounced, arrested, and executed without trial. The Roman Catholic Church was openly attacked, but the majority of people remained devoutly Catholic.

In efforts to win Polish support, the Soviet regime promoted free education and social security. Cheap books were published that were available to all, and food costs were subsidized. But the failure of the Soviet's Six-Year Plan (1950–55), which focused on developing heavy industry and collectivizing agriculture, created increasing economic disaster and social discontent. Industrial workers rioted in Poznan with the slogan "No bread without freedom."

## THE BEGINNING OF FREEDOM

October 19, 1956, marked a showdown between Poland's and Russia's Communist party leaders, Wladyslaw Gomulka and Nikita Khrushchev. Gomulka, who refused to be bullied into subservience to Russia's Communist hierarchy, was reelected that day in Warsaw as the first secretary. The only remaining Communist of importance still popular in Poland, he received messages of support from miners, steelworkers, and labor unions. He needed all the help he could muster.

Russian troops had surrounded Warsaw. Top Russian officials had flown in and were at the Belvedere Palace, where the reelection took place. The crowd at the event witnessed the confrontation between the two leaders, as Khrushchev threatened to use force if Gomulka did not comply with Russia's demands. Gomulka responded by telling the crowd what those demands were. He reminded the Russians of the economic collapse, growing Polish resentment, Russian economic exploitation, and Russia's failure to repatriate some 500,000 Poles held captive since the war.

Early the next morning, the negotiations drew to a close. A weary Gomulka told his supporters to go home, as the Russians left Warsaw. The Poles went wild, and cheering crowds filled the streets. Gomulka presented the nation with a virtual declaration of independence from Russia: "Poland has the right to be sovereign, and this sovereignty must be respected."

But by summer, the economic crisis had become so acute that the government could not maintain food subsidies. Price increases were proposed, leading to strikes and protests, which were met by police brutality and arrests. About 2,000 people were detained, many savagely beaten in custody.

*"We possess nothing—except our past."*

*—a common Polish sentiment during Communist rule*

*"This is a powder keg, and it may blow up on us at any time, but Poland is where I belong."*

*—a Pole who returned in 1956*

## AFTER THE EXCITEMENT

Gomulka had gained three concessions: the Church's independence, freedom from state-controlled agriculture, and some political freedom. But Polish Communism resulted in near starvation for much of Poland. A food price hike in 1970 drove Polish workers to strike, and a proposed price increase in 1976 provoked more strikes.

In 1980 another attempt was made to raise food prices to a more sustainable level. Shipyard strikes paralyzed the country, forcing the authorities to give in to the workers' demands for wage increases, free labor unions, and the release of political prisoners. It was a severe embarrassment to the government. Concessions reluctantly offered by the deputy prime minister were not approved by the Politburo, the Communist party's principal policy-making and executive committee. Members of the workers' opposition, the Workers Defense Committee, were detained; the editor of *Robotnik* (*The Worker*), an underground publication, was arrested and beaten. With most of the Baltic coast workforce on strike by then, the government recognized Solidarity, an organization of free trade unions.

## SOLIDARITY LIVES!

Solidarity (Solidarnosc) was the first free labor union in the Communist bloc. In December 1981, General Wojciech Jaruzelski (who earlier that year succeeded Edward Gierek, who in 1970 succeeded Gomulka) declared martial law and banned Solidarity. Its members were arrested or killed, and its leader, Lech Walesa, was locked up in a remote hunting lodge. Meanwhile, food shortages increased countrywide.

The democratic Western world thought that if the Polish Communist government could be destabilized, the collapse of Soviet dominance in

People line up to buy meat, as food shortages increase countrywide during the Solidarity-led struggle for democracy.

Eastern Europe would be hastened. The key to this was Solidarity. The Vatican and the United States supported Solidarity financially and with communication equipment, such as printing presses, shortwave radios, fax machines, and computers.

Solidarity intercepted national radio and television programming with resistance messages, ending Communist control of the mass media. In one such interception, at a national soccer championship, a banner with the words "Solidarity lives!" appeared on screen at halftime, and a message was broadcast calling for resistance.

In June 1983 John Paul II visited Poland, his second visit to his homeland after being elected pope in 1978. In July the Military Council for National Salvation, led by Jaruzelski, was dissolved; the following year thousands of political prisoners were released. In 1988 Solidarity led worker strikes across the country demanding political dialogue. Weeks of negotiation among the government, the union, and the Church led to a historic accord in 1989 that legally reinstated Solidarity and paved the way for opposition politics and free elections. The state media monopoly was lifted, and a new constitution was adopted.

# LECH WALESA

Lech Walesa (*right*) was born in 1943. At age 7, he started walking a mile to the village school everyday. He was a spirited student and loved to argue with his teachers. He hated farming and wanted to be an engineer, but his parents could not afford to send him to college. Walesa took a part-time job while attending courses at a trade school. During his military service, he was recommended for promotion, but Walesa did not choose to become a military leader.

Already known as a skilled worker, in 1967 he found a job at the gigantic Lenin Shipyards in Gdansk. At work he laid electric cables in fishing boats; at home, in a cramped house shared with three other workers, he listened to Radio Free Europe and talked politics. In 1969 Walesa married Danuta Golos, whom he met in a flower shop a year earlier.

With the economy worsening, shipyard workers got less time to do a job and no extra pay. Productivity did not increase, and in 1970 new price increases were announced. Strikes erupted all along the Baltic coast, and Walesa was at the head of a column of protesters. From then on, his life was filled with speeches to fellow workers and reasoned, if heated, arguments with his employers, and later with government representatives. When a worker with 30 years' service at the shipyard was fired in 1980 for distributing political pamphlets, general indignation sparked off a strike demanding a free labor union, free speech, and the right to strike. Feeling strongly that God was on their side, Walesa negotiated a successful settlement, and Solidarity was born.

More years of political turmoil followed. Walesa was spurned, praised, arrested, imprisoned —until in 1983 he was awarded the Nobel Peace Prize for his efforts. That brought added international prestige. He led negotiations in 1989 that resulted in Poland's first non-Communist government in 40 years. By that time, Walesa and his family were living in a large villa in Gdansk. Polish workers cheered him still but saw that he was dressed better than they were, getting a little fat, and suffering from back problems. He was tired and told them, "You have to create a couple of new Walesas. I did my part." But fate had yet another part in store for him. In 1990, nine years after he and his movement had been banned, Walesa became president of Poland.

In 1995 Walesa founded the Lech Walesa Institute to, among other goals, protect Polish independence and strengthen Polish democracy and free-market economics. Walesa has written several books and remains active in European and global social and political life.

# THE IRON CURTAIN TORN

In 1989 Poles voted in their first free elections in more than 40 years. Solidarity won all the Sejm seats that it was entitled to contest and all but one of the Senate seats. A coalition government was formed, with Tadeusz Mazowiecki as prime minister and Jaruzelski as president. But the new government faced the old economic problems: serious under-investment and poor industry and productivity. Foreign investment was sought, a stock exchange opened, and the Polish currency devalued.

In 1990 Jaruzelski stepped down, and Walesa won the presidential election. The new government elected Jan Bielecki as prime minister. But after years of one-party rule, Poland's new political problem was having too many parties, none of which were strong enough to govern alone. Successive ministers tried in vain to gain enough support from the different parties in the Sejm to form a strong base for governing. In 1993 Walesa decided to dissolve the fragmented Sejm.

The party that seemed to answer most Poles' political desires was the Democratic Left Alliance, led by Aleksander Kwasniewski, a former Communist. Kwasniewski beat Walesa in the 1995 presidential election, and in 2000 he was reelected.

In 1999 Poland joined NATO and began fulfilling obligations during the crisis in the former Yugoslavia. In 2003 members of the Polish government supported the U.S. invasion of Iraq, and Poland led 9,000 soldiers (2,000 its own) as a multinational stabilization force in south-central Iraq. In 2004, along with nine other nations, Poland joined the European Union and, recognizing that the transition from a centrally controlled economy to a more free-market system would be costly and time-consuming, began the process of integration in stages according to an agreed schedule.

A bank in Poland.

# GOVERNMENT

IN TRUE MEDIEVAL TRADITION, government in Poland began with the nobility and the peasants. The "lord of the castle" made the laws, and the peasants obeyed them. One such local leader founded the Piast dynasty, from which Poland's first kings came. Power in Europe was a constant struggle between the state and the church. The Jagiellonian dynasty dominated the 15th and 16th centuries, when Poland became more prosperous, and wealthy merchants joined the nobles as powers in the land.

In 1493 a parliament, the Sejm, was established, in which the nobility sought to curb the powers of the king and of one another. In the 16th century, the Sejm agreed that all decisions had to be unanimous and adopted the *liberum veto*, in which one member's vote was all that was needed to stop the passage of legislation. Between 1696 and 1733, use of the veto became an epidemic, and the Polish nobility agreed on nothing.

## THE FIRST CONSTITUTION

Officially called Rzeczpospolita Polska (Zhech-pos-POL-ita POL-ska), or Republic of Poland, Poland was the first country in Europe to have a constitution. The United States adopted its constitution only four years earlier. Poland's Constitution Day, May 3, 1791, is an annual holiday.

Poland's constitution introduced the concept of the sovereignty of a people, including the middle classes as well as the nobility. Political and judicial power was separated. Government was delegated to a cabinet responsible to the Sejm. Cities were allowed self-determination, and the peasants gained legal protection. Unfortunately, Poland's constitution was abolished in 1793, after the invasion by neighboring Russia.

*Opposite:* **The presidential palace in Warsaw since 1994. In the courtyard is a statue of Prince Jozef Poniatowski, nephew of King Stanislaus II.**

# REBIRTH OF DEMOCRACY

The rebirth of Polish democracy is forever enshrined in the Round Table Agreement hammered out in 1989. Solidarity won the June elections, and in September Poland had its first non-Communist government since the late 1940s.

A 100-seat Senate (upper house) was formed with the power to veto decisions made by the Sejm (lower house). The Sejm could overrule the Senate's veto only with a two-thirds majority vote.

Wojciech Jaruzelski was elected president. The Communist nominee for prime minister, Czeslaw Kiszczak, could not get enough support to form a coalition government. Solidarity's Tadeusz Mazowiecki was elected prime minister in August. But this was not the same Solidarity that had captured the imagination of the world in 1980 and 1981, when it represented the hopes of the Polish people. Now it triumphed largely because Poles refused to vote for the Communists.

In 1990 Poland tried to make its transition from a totalitarian system to a pluralist democracy and a free-market economy. Lech Walesa was democratically elected president of the republic, but domestic politics became more turbulent. Food prices rose by almost 600 percent, some state monopolies were broken up, and unemployment reached 1.3 million. Censorship and the state mass media monopoly were ended. Registering a new political party became legal and easy. The security service was disbanded.

**Poles at the polls. The ballot box is white and red, the national colors. Poles call electioneering promises intended to attract votes *kielbasa wyborcza* (kyew-BA-sa vy-BOR-cha), or election sausages.**

In early 1991 the Sejm rejected President Walesa's proposed constitutional amendments. Voters eventually faced an election with 67 political parties. Of these, 29 parties won at least one seat, but more than half of eligible voters did not vote.

## THE LAW

The Polish judicial system under Communist rule was headed by a supreme court appointed by the Council of State. The political leaders of the country appointed all judges. "Justice" went hand in hand with "politics," and that meant the official Communist doctrine.

That allegiance changed as soon as Communism died, but the legal system of a country cannot change so quickly. Poland's courts do not operate on a jury system. Every case is heard by a professional judge and two lay assessors, who are ordinary citizens elected by the local councils.

There are two categories of courts. The district courts handle most cases, civil and criminal, with serious cases being sent on to the county courts. The supreme court, located in the capital, is the country's chief judicial body.

Polish law is based on the constitution. This offers protection to the family as a unit, especially when children are involved. Small cases, such as driving offenses, are dealt with by local misdemeanor boards, whose members are elected from the local population.

Poland's restitution law aims to make reparation to Poles whose property was confiscated by the Nazis or the Communist state. The court system must sift through countless claims—from families forcefully removed from their homes to heirs of murdered Jews—to compensate rightful property owners on the value of their lost land and buildings.

## GOVERNMENT TODAY

Poland was a People's Republic from 1952 to 1989, when it became the Republic of Poland. Polish democracy continued to evolve through the 1990s. In 1997 Poland adopted a new constitution guaranteeing all its citizens basic rights that are common to most European and North American constitutions and that conform to the European Convention on Human Rights. The constitution also spells out the role of local government and of nongovernmental organizations in the process of forming stable democratic institutions.

Poland's constitution formalizes a government with three branches: executive, legislative, and judiciary.

**EXECUTIVE** power is shared by the president of the country and the Council of Ministers. The president is the head of state and the supreme commander of the armed forces. He is elected to a five-year term and works closely with the prime minister, who heads the council. The president has the duty to ensure the nation's commitment to its own constitution and to international treaties, and the power to call for parliamentary elections and to propose or veto legislation.

The main work of running the government and writing laws is the responsibility of the Council of Ministers and their leader. The prime minister is appointed by the president and approved by the Sejm, and is thus usually a member of the party that controls the majority of seats in the Sejm.

**LEGISLATIVE** power is shared by two independent elected bodies: the Sejm and the Senate. The 460-seat Sejm is the main house, with most of the authority to debate and pass laws.

*Local government in Poland is organized in 16 provinces called voivodships. The next levels of government are the powiat (pov-ee-at), or county, and the gmina (gmeen-a), or township.*

Members of both the Sejm and the 100-seat Senate serve four-year terms. The Senate, with fewer powers than the Sejm, functions in a supervisory and advisory role. The Senate can comment on and amend laws written by the Sejm, but the Sejm can override the Senate's decisions with a simple majority vote.

**JUDICIAL** authority is split among three offices: the Supreme Court, the Constitutional Tribunal, and the State Tribunal.

The Supreme Court is the highest court. It has more than 100 judges, recommended by the National Judicial Council, which consists of 24 judges serving four-year terms, and appointed by the country's president. They serve for an indefinite period. The Sejm appoints the first president of the Supreme Court on the recommendation of the country's president.

The Supreme Court, with its four chambers (civil; criminal; labor, social security, and public affairs; and military), supervises the common, military, and administrative courts, and is the court of appeal against judgments made in the lower courts.

The Constitutional Tribunal has 15 judges, selected by the Sejm for nine-year terms. They make judgments on the constitutionality of laws and their execution by government bodies.

The State Tribunal rules on constitutional or legal infringements by officials holding the highest positions in government. It has the power to remove officials from public office and to prevent candidates from holding office or voting.

**President Aleksander Kwasniewski speaks at the opening of the Sejm in 2001.**

# ECONOMY

POLAND WAS THE FIRST country in central Europe to recover from recession after ridding itself of Communism. In January 1990, the new government responded to the nation's collapsing industrial output and skyrocketing prices with a "shock therapy" program that won support from the International Monetary Fund (IMF).

The "shock therapy" program implemented by Leszek Balcerowicz, then the new finance minister, aimed for a rapid transformation of the Polish economy from central planning to free market. The currency was devalued, price controls removed, wages frozen, and state monopolies privatized. But the sudden, drastic reforms brought about great hardship, as the country suffered high unemployment and inflation rates, and shortages of goods. The economy continued to shrink in the next two years, and many Poles lived in poverty.

The turning point came in 1992. With rising foreign investment and a growing private sector, Poland became one of central Europe's strongest economies in the 1990s. But by 2001 growth had slowed. Industries such as coal and steel needed restructuring, and the government had significant ownership of the economy. New reforms aimed to restructure such industries and improve Poland's investment climate, communication and transportation networks, and living and working conditions.

A member of the World Trade Organization (WTO) and of the European Union (EU), Poland remains active in international trade, with healthy prospects for continued economic growth.

*Opposite:* **Cafés and shops line Warsaw's trendy New World, or Nowy Swiat, boulevard.**

*Below:* **Bricklayers in a church courtyard.**

## *AGRICULTURE*

Poland, with around 10 million farms employing around one quarter of the workforce, is a leading agricultural producer. Wheat, rye, potatoes, sugar beets, and fruit are important crops. Polish farms also raise cattle, sheep, and hogs.

Having been under Soviet domination for so long, Poland is unusual for having more than 75 percent of its farmland privately owned. Most family farms in Poland are tiny compared to similar farms in other EU countries. And without the state subsidies they received on fuel and materials during the Communist era, many private farms in Poland are economically unsound. Modern machinery is used where it can be afforded, but horses are still used to power the work on some farms. Most small farmers produce for their family's consumption more than to sell for money.

As Poland integrates into the European Union, Polish farmers face the biggest changes in hundreds of years. They now compete against multinational agribusiness concerns. Farmers who are able to adapt will become richer than their predecessors. Most are probably destined to leave the land of their ancestors and seek their livelihood in other ways.

## *MINING*

Hard coal is abundant in Poland, especially in the Upper Silesia region. There are also large reserves of brown coal, or lignite. Coal is used to generate most of Poland's energy and is a major export. Poland is one of the biggest coal producers in the world. The Polish coal industry has been the focus of restructuring and privatization efforts since the 1990s. Many of the country's coal mines have been closed down because they were inefficient and unprofitable.

Some of the world's largest deposits of sulfur are found in Poland, especially near the city of Tarnobrzeg in the southeast. The region is a special economic zone that attracts investors with technical infrastructure and provides employment for the region's inhabitants. Most of Poland's sulfur exports head for other European countries. Copper and rock salt are two other minerals commercially extracted in Poland.

## MANUFACTURING

Poland manufactures steel, chemicals, glass, paper, washing machines, refrigerators, televisions, and motor vehicles, among other products. When many of its industrial areas were set up, more than half the output went to the Soviet Union or other Communist countries. Now most Polish exports go to countries in the European Union and Southeast Asia.

Many of Poland's shipyards were destroyed in World War II, and it was not until 1949 that Poland's first postwar ocean-going vessel was launched. Under state control, Poland's shipbuilding industry changed from steam to diesel power. In the 1970s, the yards were modified with new technology. The Lenin Shipyards in Gdansk could boast a steady output of factory ships from fishing vessels and ferries to container and bulk-cargo carriers. At the start of the 21st century, however, the shipbuilding industry has been plagued with corruption and fiscal mismanagement, and it looks as though foreign investors will buy out what could have been an important industry for the "new" Poland.

## SHOPPING

During the 40 years of Communist control, Poles stood in long lines to buy the most basic products, such as food and clothes. Shopping could take all day. The expression *niema* (NYE-ma), meaning there is none, became almost a joke.

Today Poles can find all the goods they could want in shops and markets, although not everyone might be able to afford them. During the economic crisis years of 1990 and 1991, the income of town workers fell by 25 percent and that of rural farmers fell by 45 percent. Family incomes have since risen slowly, but they remain low. The average monthly salary in 2002 was around $430, compared to less than $150 in 1991. Households in the cities generally earn more than households in the rural areas.

In 1992 prices of consumer goods rose by 40 percent, so most housewives spent time comparing prices before buying anything. Most traveled by bus, and their favorite conversation topic was where the best bargains could be found. Food used up 45 percent of their weekly pay, clothes 10 percent.

Shopping malls are being built on the outskirts of larger cities. Major European brands are now available to urbanites in Poland. There are also hypermarkets on the outskirts of Warsaw and in many other major cities. For bargain hunters, the best places to go are the bazaars. In Warsaw, hundreds of petty traders "set up shop" on weekends in front of the huge department-store buildings, in the shadow of the Palace of Culture and Science. The largest bazaar is in the former national stadium in the capital city's eastern Praga district. The bazaars sell clocks, watches, antique furniture, paintings, and everyday items such as toys, clothes and shoes, fruit and vegetables.

The bazaars are a vital source of extra income not only for Poles but also people from neighboring countries. Whether this is smuggling or "trade tourism" depends on your point of view. The practice began in 1989 when Poles, allowed into West Berlin, flooded in with vodka at half the usual price, found ready customers, and loaded up with goods to sell back home. Warsaw's bazaars, though declining, remain popular among traders and tourists.

**An informal Polish market forms as women sell goods at the subway.**

## TRADE UNIONS

Under Communist rule, efficiency was not considered as important as full employment. What mattered to Poles was a wage sufficient to feed their families. The slogan "Good Bread for Good Work" was coined in 1980 when the government attempted to raise food prices drastically without raising wages.

In December 1970, workers were killed in front of the gates of the Lenin Shipyards in Gdansk when they wanted to protest against price increases. The Politburo sent tanks to stop the thousands of marchers. A decade later, in the same place, 37-year-old Lech Walesa was elected chairman of a new labor union independent of the state. The union, called Solidarity, came after two free trade unions founded in 1978 in Silesia and Gdansk.

Solidarity changed into a political movement. Eleven citizen committees formed to represent the opposition to Communist rule, and in the elections of June 1989, Tadeusz Mazowiecki (editor-in-chief of the Solidarity newspaper) headed the first freely elected non-Communist government in the Warsaw Pact of Communist-controlled countries.

Solidarity's success inspired people-power movements elsewhere in Eastern Europe.

## THE SOVIET LEGACY

The industrial projects so energetically started during Communist rule were either poorly sited—as in the case of the Katowice steel complex in Silesia 1,250 miles (2,012 km) away from its ore supply in the Soviet Union—or uneconomical because of an oversupply in the world steel market. Debts mounted. Poland could not repay what it had borrowed, because it could not sell its products to the West. In desperation, food products, raw materials, and fuel were sold abroad, causing acute shortages at home. In 1980 Poland suspended its repayment of foreign loans; that led to a foreign debt of $43 billion by 1990.

The trouble was that one often had to resort to dire means of subsistence in order to provide for the family's needs. Workers in factories took wagonloads of coal; clerks in state-owned shops took and resold merchandise; and tax collectors accepted bribes. A Communist deputy once calculated that everyday about $120,000 was handed out in bribes and just under one million dollars' worth of merchandise stolen. Poles became accustomed to shrugging off any qualms at "cheating the government."

## PROBLEMS OF A FREED MARKET

In 1989, the year of political reform, the inflation rate exceeded 600 percent. Wide-ranging measures were passed to convert to a market-oriented economic system. Price subsidies were abolished, the zloty (Poland's currency) substantially devalued, foreign investment encouraged, and state enterprises transferred to private ownership.

Swiftly, industry declined by 30 percent, sales of domestic products by 37 percent, and real wages by 33 percent. By the end of 1990, the recession had slowed, but real income remained 30 percent below the 1989 level. Whereas in the Communist era, unemployment had been officially stated as zero, it now stood at 1.3 million, or 8 percent of the workforce. The World Bank approved loans of $900 million to boost exports and natural-gas production and to build up a market economy.

In 1991 Poland had a foreign debt of $35 billion. The 17 European nations that had loaned money to Poland agreed to write off a sizable portion of Poland's debt on condition that Poland followed an International Monetary Fund (IMF) program to stabilize its economy. The United States also agreed to cut Poland's debt by 70 percent. Germany and France had already made similar debt reductions in support of Poland's transition to democracy. In return, Poland made harsh cuts to government spending on social projects and welfare benefits.

Poland's economy has grown slowly but steadily since the 1990s. Foreign investment has increased, and inflation decreased. However, chronic underemployment and unemployment continue to plague the country. The hope is that as Poland integrates into the European Union, a market of almost half a billion people, new opportunities will emerge for Polish goods and services. Until then, more economic and social displacement is likely to occur.

*"We, too, will one day be efficient. But we have to fire all our planners first."*

*—An old Polish saying*

## THE MARKETPLACE OF TOMORROW

Poland presents great opportunities for private enterprise. Foreign companies such as Coca-Cola, Unilever, and Fiat set up plants in the country in the early 1990s. Fresh into the next decade, Poland found its telecommunication industry the object of intense competition for ownership by foreign companies such as France Telecom and Deutsche Telekom. Poland's biggest U.S. investors include Citigroup, General Motors, Procter & Gamble, and Epstein, in industries such as financial services, automobiles, sanitary products, and building construction.

But Poland's integration into European trading circles has been difficult. Polish steel, for example, is not in high demand, since the European Union produces more steel than its members need. Also, Poland's outdated Communist-era steel mills have a long way to go in improving their productivity levels to catch up with those in more developed EU nations. Under the pressures of output reductions and structural changes, Poland's steel industry has seen the loss of tens of thousands of jobs.

EU membership in 2004 gave Poland access to centralized funds accumulated from tax revenues and member contributions. These finance farm incomes, infrastructural and social development, health services, and education programs in the European Union and provided economic relief during Poland's disruptive phase of industrial restructuring. The hope is that the construction of transportation networks, and access to administrative expertise from the European Union will bring development to even the smallest communities.

This Athlete's Foot store in Krakow is a U.S. franchise for sports goods.

# ENVIRONMENT

MORE THAN 40 YEARS of Communist rule have scarred the natural environment of Poland and its neighbors. The Communist authorities, who showed even less environmental concern than did their more democratic counterparts in Western Europe and North America, made economic decisions that would have long-term consequences for the environment and people.

The situation is not much different in post-Communist Poland. The barriers to environmental conservation initiatives remain economic. Logging, for instance, threatens the survival of the Bialowieza Forest that lies outside the Bialowieza National Park. Activists have since 1994 been campaigning for the enlargement of the national park, which protects only a small section of the forest. But theirs is a mammoth task, since logging remains one of the few profitable industries in a region of high unemployment.

As transportation networks penetrate previously inaccessible areas, modern highways will connect Poland to Western Europe. But such development will divide virgin forests and push wildlife into ever-shrinking refuges.

As Poland integrates into the European Union, laws and regulations need to be formulated and refined to protect the country's fragile ecosystems from a surge of urbanization and industrial development. Manufacturing plants have to upgrade their facilities and equipment in order to reduce the amount of harmful substances they release into the air and waterways.

Funds from the European Union's budget finance the building of community infrastructure and waste-disposal facilities to support the progress Poland is making in cleaning up its natural environment.

*Here, nature soundly sleeping Never hears the human tread, Here the elements nap in silence Like unspooked wild animals, Whose herds do not take flight At the sight of a human face.*

*—from* Farys *(1828), written by Polish poet Adam Mickiewicz (1798–1855)*

*Opposite:* **A stream in the forest of the Strazyska valley in the Polish Tatras.**

## *AIR POLLUTION*

Poland's abundant reserves of brown coal are its main source of fuel, generating 98 percent of Poland's electrical supply. Brown coal is also burned to supply towns and cities with heat during the winter months. Travelers to Poland are often warned about the poor air quality in the country during winter.

Industrial activity has also raised the presence of sulfur dioxide, nitrogen oxides, carbon dioxide, dust, heavy metals, and hydrocarbons in the air to harmful levels. Most parts of Poland are affected by this pollution, but the Upper Silesia region suffers the most. It is Poland's

**An aerial view of Warsaw city. The air in the cities tends to be degraded by traffic emissions.**

mining center and hosts much of the country's heavy industrial activity. The Upper Silesia region accounts for approximately a quarter of the country's emissions of sulfur dioxide, nitrogen oxides, and dust. When these gases combine with moisture in the air, acid rain forms. It has depleted forests in the nearby Karkonosze and Izerskie mountains.

Air pollution in the Upper Silesia region has affected the health of people living there. For years, the region had a mortality rate that was higher than the national average, and there was a high incidence of children being born underweight. Birth defects are more common in Upper Silesia than in the rest of Poland.

Vehicular emissions contribute substantially to air pollution in the capital and other cities, especially around major road intersections. Of all particles released, heavy metals such as lead are the most harmful. Car ownership started to rise after Communism fell. In Warsaw, road congestion became a problem, only partially relieved when the subway system, Metro Warszawskie, was opened in 1995. Improving transportation networks is an ongoing challenge as cityscapes in Poland continue to morph and transform.

**DEALING WITH AIR POLLUTION**  The closure of inefficient factories and mines after Poland became fully independent was economically motivated, but the action had a positive environmental side effect: it removed some major sources of air pollution.

Nevertheless, the environment ministry has taken formal steps to improve air quality, setting limits on a variety of pollutants. Old power plants have had to drastically reduce their emissions, and new plants are being built according to stringent codes.

Poland has adopted EU air-quality standards and has been receiving aid to meet those standards.

Absorbing contaminants
from the many cities on
its banks, the Vistula
River is a major polluter
of the Baltic Sea.

## *WATER POLLUTION*

Despite having so many rivers, many communities in Poland lack clean water due to the poor planning of the Communist government. Because of the high cost associated with equipping existing communities with sewage treatment facilities, the current government has been slow in addressing water pollution in the country.

As late as 1995, many Polish factories and cities had no sewage treatment facility. Most homes in the villages receive a water supply, but few are connected to proper sewer systems. Most of the country's river water is seriously contaminated. Expensive wells that go deep into the earth are used to produce potable water. The water of the Vistula River cannot be used for irrigation.

Most Poles are aware of the environmental challenges that face the nation. A network of organizations—national and international, private and government—actively work to make Polish land, air, water, and people healthier.

## PRESERVATION EFFORTS

Poland's environment ministry oversees departments and offices with different areas of responsibility, such as forestry, water resources, nature conservation, and environmental education and communication. Poland has signed international agreements on concerns ranging from climate change and the ozone layer, to biodiversity and endangered species.

Polish nongovernmental environmental groups work within their industries to influence decisions with environmental implications, or campaign directly against destructive actions. The Polish Ecological Club is one such group.

The World Conservation Union (IUCN) and the World Wildlife Fund (WWF) are among the international organizations that maintain a presence in Poland to protect the country's natural heritage.

**Recycling bins near Krakow's Cloth Hall create an atmospheric blend of centuries-old economic activity and modern-day environmental awareness.**

## *EUROPE'S NATURAL HISTORY*

Some of Poland's wildlife has adapted to the changing landscape. The white stork, which migrates each spring to Poland, is one example. It does not need trees to nest but will build its nest on a roof.

Fortunately, in Poland this is considered good luck. A Polish saying goes: "If a stork builds a nest on your roof, your focus shall be a happy family life." Each year, the return of the migrating storks is awaited and announced in the mass media. In many places special nesting poles are even erected to attract storks.

Unlike the stork, Poland's rare animals are struggling to survive as human activity shrinks their natural habitat. Poland's national parks protect the country's endangered species. The oldest of the parks is part of the Bialowieza Forest, the last section of a primeval forest that covered

**Lambs in Zakopane.**

most of Europe's lowlands thousands of years ago. The forest extends across the border into Belarus, making it one of the most important natural refuges in Europe. It shelters one of Europe's most precious animals—the European bison. Poaching and hunting decimated many bison populations in the 1800s. The biggest free-range herbivore in Europe, the bison eats ferns, lichens, mosses, and the bark and leaves of trees. It can grow to more than 1,700 pounds (770 kg) in weight. Bulls tend to live alone, except during the mating season. The European bison was gradually reintroduced in the wild in the 1900s. Today, most live in the Bialowieza Forest.

The Tatra National Park has as its symbol the chamois, also protected under Polish law. The Bialowieza, Kampinos, and Tatra national parks are all UNESCO biosphere reserves. They are conservation areas that support sustainable development as well as international sharing of environmental research findings. The European lynx, for a while absent from its historical habitat in the Polish lowlands, has been reintroduced in Poland, particularly in the Kampinos National Park, where it lives as a protected species. Elk and European beaver are two other mammals that have been successfully reintroduced in Kampinos.

The Baltic Sea is home to the harbor porpoise, whose numbers have decreased drastically due largely to accidental capture in fishing nets. The porpoise is a mammal like the whale and dolphin but is smaller and has no beak. The harbor porpoise rises to breathe every few minutes when feeding. It eats fish and can grow up to 145 pounds (65 kg) in weight.

Poland works with other signatories to the Agreement on the Conservation of Small Cetaceans of the Baltic and North Seas, to strengthen international law on the killing of such animals, to monitor their population and food supply, to reduce pollution in the seas, and to improve fishing practices.

# POLES

THE PEOPLE of the first Polish kingdom were called Polani—people of the fields—and agriculture is still important. Many rural farmers still farm using traditional methods including scythes and horse-drawn plows.

Poland today is the most homogeneous state in Europe. The Polish people originate from one race. They are almost all Slavs and speak the same language with some regional differences. And they are almost all Roman Catholics.

Their Slavic heritage gives the Poles generally light-colored hair and eyes and a slightly dark complexion. Intermarriages that occurred during the nation's history of foreign invasions have resulted in a population with diverse physical characteristics.

Poland's population is one of the youngest in Europe. Seventeen percent of its more than 38.6 million people are under age 15. Border movements in the past displaced Germans, Ukrainians, Belarusians, and Lithuanians living near Poland's borders. These peoples established minority communities that today, along with other, smaller minority groups, make up less than 5 percent of the population. Jews number around 8,000, mostly in Warsaw. Before World War II, Poland had Europe's largest Jewish community—more than 3 million.

On the other hand, there are Poles living in Ukraine, Belarus, and Lithuania. Poles who were forced to leave their homeland for political or economic reasons include the thousands who, during World War II, lost their lands and were sent to Kazakhstan and Siberia, where they were forbidden to speak Polish or talk about what had happened to them. Yet other Poles left on their own will, settling in the United States, Canada, and Western European countries. It is estimated that the Polish diaspora is 20-million strong.

*Opposite:* **Polish youths at a festival.**

## MINORITY GROUPS

A little Polish girl happily wears her nation's traditional dress, which is popular at festivals.

Magyar horsemen swept through Poland in the ninth century. Mongol horsemen invaded in the 13th century. The Polish king subsequently opened his country to outsiders if they would come and repopulate its devastated lands. Millions came, including Jews fleeing persecution in other parts of Europe. Fifteenth- and 16th-century Poland was a country of religious tolerance. There were nearly 100 mosques in the country and synagogues in most towns. Shifting borders through the centuries resulted in small pockets of ethnic minorities being left inside or outside Poland. When from 1919 to 1921 the borders of the Second Republic were drawn, Poland was the sixth largest territory in Europe, with ethnic minorities totalling some 9 million—about a third of the population.

**UKRAINIANS** When the borders changed yet again in 1945, there were some 700,000 Ukrainians living in Poland. Some moved reluctantly to what became the Ukrainian Soviet Socialist Republic. Most preferred to stay and fought for the right to. By 1947 the Polish authorities decided to send the remaining 200,000 Ukrainians elsewhere. Most were sent to the west, where there were empty farms left by the Germans, but no more than two or three Ukrainian families were ever allowed to settle in the same village.

Deliberately separated by the Communists, some 300,000 Ukrainians in Poland today struggle to maintain their traditions. Only one primary school and two high schools offer Ukrainian language courses. Efforts are being made to conserve their churches, which have fallen into disrepair. The Festival of Ukrainian Culture at Sopot, where choirs and dance groups celebrate with true Ukrainian music, is held only once in two years.

**BELARUSIANS**  Around 170,000 Belarusians live in the east of Poland, mostly around the Bialystok area. Near Siemiatycze is the Holy Mount of Grabarka, where Belarusian pilgrims, of the old Orthodox Church, climb carrying crosses to the summit. A Belarusian Democratic Union was founded in 1990 to represent the interests of Poland's Belarusian community.

**LITHUANIANS**  Around 10,000 Lithuanians live in the Punsk area near the Polish border with Lithuania. Punsk has the only Lithuanian school in Poland, and it is also where Poland's Lithuanian community runs a few societies and centers to promote their culture and language and tighten their community.

**GERMANS**  Poland's German minority is concentrated in the Silesia region. The Potsdam Conference of 1945 approved the repatriation of Germans, who were replaced by Poles returning home from exile or imprisonment in the Soviet Union and other countries. So people in the west and southwest are not all descended from original Polish inhabitants. Many are of pure German ancestry.

*"Poland is our homeland, but it does not belong only to Poles. We share this country with people of other nationalities."*

*—Tadeusz Mazowiecki, in his inaugural speech as prime minister, September 1989*

## POLISH JEWS

The first Jews to settle in Poland probably came from beyond the Volga River, an area that had established Judaism as a state religion in the eighth century. When Jews were expelled from other European countries in the Middle Ages, they were accepted in Poland. They were allowed to cultivate their culture and customs. In 1939 there were about 3.5 million Jews in Poland—about 10 percent of the country's population. Doctors, teachers, scientists, industrialists, bankers, and businessmen—they were accepted by all. The meat trade was virtually run by them.

Most Polish Jews, especially the lower classes who were tailors and cobblers, were Orthodox Jews and vehemently anti-Communist. More important, they wanted to be left alone. So the violence of the Nazi occupation, during which almost the entire Jewish population was deliberately exterminated, remains a horrific chapter in Polish history. There are only some 5,000 Polish Jews left from their former millions. Their only distinguishing factor is their religion. The national identity is closely tied with Catholicism, so many Polish Jews see themselves somehow different. They run their own organizations and schools, and there is a Jewish theater in Warsaw and a Jewish Historical Institute with its own library and museum.

A Jewish cemetery in Warsaw.

## THE GORALE

Not a minority group but an identity group, Polish highlanders, known as the Gorale (goor-A-le), are an independent-minded people with a distinctive mountain way of life. The Gorale live in the Podhale region in the Tatra Mountains. Traditionally pastoralists, they raise sheep and goats, growing only a few crops, such as oats, barley, or potatoes.

With access to more modern agricultural methods today, the Gorale have ventured into dairy farming. The men do the work that involves the use of horses, machines, and tools such as scythes, while the women and children rake, turn hay, plant and gather potatoes, and weed the vegetables.

Most Gorale live in small villages of wooden houses surrounded by long strip fields, pastures, and forest. There is a growing tendency for young couples to establish a new household, but the three-generation extended family is still common. Two-room wooden huts stand beside modern multi-story brick houses. But even in the modern houses, families tend to live, eat, and sleep in one or two rooms while renting the other rooms to tourists.

The Podhale has several market towns and a few resorts. One of the poorest areas in Poland, it is now benefiting from the tourist dollar.

The Gorale are strongly and uniformly Catholic. For them, religious events are the most important annual events. Every Easter, Christmas, and May (the month the Virgin Mary's ascent into heaven is celebrated), the churches and shrines are beautifully decorated. The old lifestyle has persisted despite years under Austrian rule, Nazi invasion, and Communist rule.

**Loggers at work in the Tatra Mountains maintain the old way of life.**

The baggy pants of Polish folk musicians suggest a Turkish influence.

## TRADITIONAL COSTUMES

In 14th-century Poland, only nobility had the right to wear red. That was how the word *karmazyn* (kar-MA-zyn), or crimson, came to mean gentleman. Poles today often wear clothes of predominantly red and white, because those are the national colors of Poland.

The *kontousch* (kon-TUSH) overgarment with slashed sleeves and its *joupane* (yo-PA-ne) undergarment of a long tunic show the influence of the Asiatic world. The style was probably copied from Persia—Poland's borders once stretched to the Black Sea. Similarly, the baggy pants and flowing cloaks of the men could have Turkish origins. Polish men traditionally wore fur caps. Peasants wore short tunics of handwoven materials in soft natural colors. They also wore long pants, a cloak of sheepskin, and boots or shoes made from woven strips of bark.

The important element is decoration: edgings in brightly contrasting materials, trimmings of colored string, red or green lapels on coats, studded belts, metal ornaments, appliqué work, and embroidery. The richest appliqué work can be seen on the leather bodices and pants in the Carpathian mountain area. Lace and crochet are made in intricate designs, especially in Silesia.

**Amber from the Baltic is greatly prized.**

Polish women delight in wearing amber bead necklaces. This was a way for a prospective bride to show off her wealth. Amber from the Baltic is increasingly precious, especially if there is a fossilized insect trapped in the resin. Coral beads are thought to bring good luck, in the form of many healthy children.

Today, such finery is reserved for Sunday dress or special festivals. On those days, women wear red and blue pleated skirts, with a richly floral blouse and, for older women, a headscarf. For the rest of the week, they wear more somber or casual clothes, such as black skirts, dark suits, or T-shirts and jeans.

Another aspect of Polish tradition is their love of horses. Horses were a symbol of warrior status. They were lovingly cared for, covered in rich cloths at parades, adorned with plumes, and dyed on special occasions. The favorite color was red, but for funerals black with a purple or green mane and tail was a popular combination. Turkish horses were crossed with European breeds, and the Polish cavalry out-numbered the infantry three to one in the 17th century.

# LIFESTYLE

"I MAY BE THE HEAD of the family, but the mother is the heart," says a true Polish father. Although both husband and wife go to work, Polish men still believe that the mother should be at home. This belief is particularly strong in Silesia, where people object strongly to husband and wife being taxed separately.

The idea of family remains important in both town and country, and parents seem to make even bigger sacrifices for their children. This emphasis on family grew stronger during the brutal years of martial law, when random searches were carried out on the streets. With many unsuspected government informers, no one knew whom to trust any more, so people retreated into their immediate family circles.

Now that four and a half decades of repressive totalitarianism have ended in Poland, the feeling is not of liberation but of venturing into an unknown freedom.

*Left:* **A family feeds the birds in the town square. The family is important whether one lives in the town or the countryside.**

*Opposite:* **For Poles living an urban lifestyle, cafés are convenient places to grab a snack or have a drink with friends.**

## POLISH PATRIOTISM

It is difficult, if not dangerous, to try to sum up national characteristics, but robust patriotism is surely the keynote to Polish character. Few can deny that Polish determination and cheerfulness have been unshakeable in the face of hardship. This has resulted in a rowdy, friendly public life. During the martial law years, when protest could lead to imprisonment, many Poles wore buttons printed with "DOWN WITH THE MILITARY JUNTA" in large letters, followed in tiny letters by "in El Salvador." It was not a very significant protest, but it was typical of the Poles' refusal to admit defeat. After the secret police were removed in 1956, freedom of speech became a Polish delight.

The Palace of Culture and Science was Stalin's gift to the Polish people.

The wry humor of the Polish people is illustrated in the way residents will explain to visitors that the best view of the city of Warsaw is from the top of the 37-story Palace of Culture and Science. Why? Because that is the only place from which you cannot see the Palace of Culture and Science! Poles thoroughly dislike this building—the "wedding-cake skyscraper"—as it was a gift from Jozef Stalin and thus symbolizes Soviet domination.

Rejoicing in their relatively newborn democracy, younger Poles (the 30-somethings) often disguise their present struggles for jobs, money, and the children's needs with stories of past horrors—how it took eight weeks to get an application form for a passport, a year for a television set; how one had to pay a bribe just to keep their place on the waiting list. Older Poles, however, remember the good old times of the 1970s,

when foreign loans gave their country access to many material goods at cheap prices.

It is their fervent nationalism that has sustained the Poles through history. Foreign invasions and partitions could not kill their instinct to survive, even when they were landless for a hundred years or when they were massacred by the Nazis. The Poles not only withstood the persecution but arose to lead their neighbors in bringing down Communism.

Polish optimism is renowned. For example, there are some who insist it never rains on Saturdays. The traditional saying goes: "Saturday is the day the Blessed Virgin does the celestial washing. Therefore it cannot rain."

The Poles are fond of their eccentricity. More than a few will tell the story of Karol Radziwill, an 18th-century Polish nobleman who was fond of drinking. Apparently, his favorite activity was shooting at bison catapulted into the air. In his chapel, music was played by an orchestra dressed as Turkish soldiers. When people criticized him for living better than the king, he said, "I live like a Radziwill. The king can live how he likes."

## POVERTY-LINE LIVING

While Poland has made significant economic progress since the fall of Communism, many Polish families still face a hard life. Apartments are easier to find now than during the days of Communist rule, when only members of the ruling party could live in more than one room. But many families still have to live in cramped apartments, because they cannot afford bigger ones. As credit-extending institutions gain respectability, more and more Poles will be able to obtain a mortgage and own better homes.

The weekend market in Warsaw has stalls selling anything and everything.

Poles are now taking advantage of modern financial institutions and services. Major U.S. and European banks operate hundreds of branches in Poland, even in the small cities. To compete, Polish banks have had to improve to become professional, dependable institutions. Gone are the days of stuffing money into socks in the chimney or into mattresses. Gone also are the days of black-market shops that supplemented the state network. There are no longer empty shelves or lines for scarce items. Shops have everything Poles need, provided they can afford it. Many still cannot.

While the middle class is growing, especially in urban areas, older people and those in the countryside continue to suffer as more communities and individuals become integrated into modern Europe.

## CHILDREN

There is a street in Warsaw called Kubus Puhatek, or Winnie the Pooh, named so at the request of children. Would any other nation take their children so seriously?

Polish children learn etiquette from an early age. Some boys are still taught to kiss a woman's hand in greeting. But gone are the days when Polish children would shower visitors with questions about "life in the West." Most Polish children have access to the same books and magazines, television and radio programs, and computer games that children in other European countries have. Polish children also dress the way their peers in the United States do and have similar ambitions. Many learn English as a second language, starting in kindergarten. Almost all are Internet savvy.

School hours were shortened when the country's economic transformation began. Many children finish the school day before their parents get home from work. There is unease about the number of kids who wander the streets with nothing worthwhile to do. Videos, DVDs, computer games, and the Internet are popular pursuits among young people.

In the Polish countryside, children dream of going to the city. Originally, they went in search of work, but now many are attracted by the modern entertainments unavailable in rural life.

The legal age in Poland is 18. Only then does a young person gain the full rights of Polish citizenship.

A group of schoolchildren visit Wawel Palace in Krakow. The Poles have a saying that a child drinks the love of Poland with his or her mother's milk.

# EDUCATION

Poles greatly value education and knowledge. As early as 1773, they established a national education commission, the first central non-religious education authority in Central Europe. It started a system of primary and secondary schools plus higher education that has lasted to today; the only addition has been pre-primary school.

Pre-primary school, for children ages 3 to 6, is not free, but from age 7, education is compulsory and free. More than 7 million children go to primary and secondary school. Poland has a 98-percent literacy rate and 97-percent school attendance.

Polish culture and history are strongly emphasized in the school curriculum, as are foreign languages and computer skills. High-school students specialize and can choose from a range of subjects, including German, English, biology, chemistry, and mathematics. Lessons last from 8 A.M. to 1 P.M. (or 2:30 P.M. at the latest).

In 2000 there were more than 1.5 million students in Polish institutions of higher learning. The number of undergraduates increased throughout the 1990s, making for tough competition to get in, as there is a limited number of places in the universities and similar institutions. Tuition is free for students accepted to university.

Poland is proud of its universities. The Jagiellonian University in Krakow was founded in 1364, making it the

Polish children in primary school.

The courtyard of the Wawel Castle.

oldest in Central Europe after the University of Prague. Two of the Jagiellonian University's most famous students are astronomer Nicolaus Copernicus and Karol Wojtyla, Pope John Paul II. The Flying University, founded in 1882, gave Polish women the chance to pursue higher education. Classes were held in people's homes and moved from one apartment to another, hence the name Flying University.

Government cost cutting has affected education in Poland. Teachers under Communist rule were accustomed to having a job for life, but now they have to produce results to keep their jobs. Reduced government spending has also meant fewer teaching hours and sometimes smaller paychecks. Schools may use a double shift, with some students studying in the morning and others in the afternoon, so that fewer teachers are needed. Tightened budgets mean that some optional classes have been discontinued. Schools have to find sponsors or engage in fund-raising activities to get extra income. The popularity of private schools has increased as they grow in number and quality. As study loans become available and people value learning more, even adults are attending classes to gain new knowledge and skills. Particularly popular are computer skills training programs.

**Flower sellers in Poland never lack customers.**

## *STATE OF HEALTH*

The Polish socialist state used to assure its citizens of full medical care at no cost. Like the bland assertion of full employment, that was only propaganda. The general health of the people was low, and medical standards were poor. Poles went to a pharmacy if they felt unwell and consulted the pharmacist there. They were reluctant to go to a hospital where there were too few beds, insufficient medicines, and sometimes unsanitary conditions.

Even today, workers in Poland's public health sector have a heavy workload, and most people cannot afford private treatment. The health ministry runs clinics, hospitals, sanatoriums, and ambulance services, but the staffs are poorly paid and the quality of treatment still leaves a lot to be desired.

The labor ministry administers a social security system that includes free medical treatment for all workers and their families, as well as for pensioners, invalids, and students. There are homes for pensioners, the chronically ill, and the mentally disabled.

## FLOWERS EVERYWHERE!

Poles love flowers. They grow them in flower beds and window boxes and on balconies. Their traditional dress designs, pottery, and woodcarvings are all flower-decked. Poppies and roses predominate, with cornflowers, marigolds, or blue and purple crocuses in the springtime.

It is a Polish custom to bring flowers when visiting someone—for birthdays, namedays, weddings, Sunday lunches, anything! Flowers also decorate cemeteries, honoring Poland's many dead. This large demand for flowers is easily supplied by flower sellers found everywhere. Bouquets of roses or carnations resplendent in a silver paper sheath are popular.

## *SPECIAL SUNDAY*

In Poland, survival is a family commitment, especially in the countryside, where children work in the fields, turning hay or tending the animals, on Saturdays or during school holidays.

But Sunday is a day of rest. For rural families, Sunday may start with a bath for everyone. Then father puts on a suit and polished pointed shoes, mother shows off a traditional dress with floral patterns, and the children are smart in clean jeans and a freshly ironed shirt with a bright scarf. The house is tidied, chores are done, and off they go to 11 o'clock Mass.

People selling flowers or local produce seize the chance to set up their stalls in the churchyard, where there will be a ready crowd after the Mass. The men will gather for a drink, and the children hang out.

But the women return home to prepare lunch. The long, leisurely Sunday afternoon includes a promenade down the main street, with youths racing their bikes through the park and couples strolling hand-in-hand and eating ice cream. Some lean out from their apartment balconies to share the sun with their friends.

On Sundays, Poles love to walk about town, ride a bike, walk in the park, or engage in a dozen other relaxing pursuits.

71

## ON THE MOVE

Car ownership in Poland has skyrocketed from the days when no one could afford to buy a car. Car dealerships were among the first institutions to lend money to people to buy on credit.

The old Communist-built automobiles, common in the 1980s and 1990s, are rare on Polish roads today. Poles have access to the variety of car models available to drivers in other parts of Western Europe.

But Poland's roads are a different matter. An important impetus to joining the European Union was that funds would become available to build highways connecting communities in Poland and elsewhere in Europe. Poland has about 155,000 miles (249,448 km) of paved highways, of which 224 miles (360 km) are expressways.

Poles love to travel, crisscrossing the country, clogging single-lane highways and often sharing them with trucks, tractors, and even horse carts. Roads in and around the smaller cities can get quite congested due to the lack of road development, and there are still cobblestone lanes in some areas.

The Polish State Railway trains are among the busiest in Europe. Commuter trains in the large cities are crowded. Buses are cheaper than trains but are also usually crowded. Private bus companies have sprung up to compete with state-run systems. Domestic flights enable easy inter-city movement.

**City traffic is a mix of streetcars, buses, and cars.**

A farming couple share the work of harvesting hay.

## COUNTRY LIFE

On the Polish plain, peasants have cultivated vegetables, wheat, and rye for centuries. During the rise and fall of great empires and the marauding of armies, it was the noble houses and the great castles that tended to be destroyed. Once peace returned, the farmers returned to work. Communists, like previous invaders, drove out the landowners, but the farmers and the priests always endured. Indeed, the clergy presides at every important family event: christenings, weddings, and funerals.

Farming families own scattered strips of land. This is the result of a complicated system of private ownership that divides land among a man's heirs. A person who marrys someone from another village can end up with scattered landholdings.

Today, thousands of rural families live on a thin strip of land with a house next to the road, then a vegetable garden, then a couple of fruit trees, and then the field, with perhaps a cow and a few chickens. The men mow the hay, and the women and children rake it. Every area has its own distinctive style of haycocks, drying the hay over wood frames or piled branches. Small towns come to life twice a week: on market day and on Sunday.

73

## TOWN LIFE

With rapid industrialization and urbanization since World War II, 60 percent of the population now live in towns. The movement of people from the expanse of the countryside to the denseness of the towns has created tremendous problems of housing and overcrowding. From the space, the quiet, and the fresh air of their farms and villages, new town dwellers found themselves looking out small apartment windows onto narrow streets.

The outskirts of Warsaw is where most Varsovians (as residents of Warsaw are called) live in uniform suburbs of rectangular blocks of apartments—a stark contrast to the beautifully restored Old Town that intrigues most visitors to Warsaw. However, not all urbanites live in grey industrial areas. New apartment blocks and clean suburbs are being built—at a price—in areas where the streets are litter-free and there is hardly any graffiti.

Poles grow fruit and vegetables on their small plots of land.

Unemployment is a major concern, as inefficient offices and mines have been closed. Countless state offices once employed more than half the urban population during the days of Communist bureaucracy. Then, it was state policy to create jobs even where there was no work. Today, many people have been put out of work because of technology and a more realistic job market.

## LIFE IN WARSAW

The outskirts of the Polish capital are a different world from the city's much-photographed Old Town. This is suburban Warsaw, where most Varsovians live in mammoth apartment blocks.

Teresa lives with her mother and father and their new puppy on the eighth floor of a tower block. They are lucky to have a small apartment with two rooms, besides a bathroom and a tiny kitchen.

Teresa is used to it. "At least we have a good view!" she says as she waters the flower pots on the balcony. Until last year, Teresa and her parents shared the apartment with grandpa and grandma.

On weekdays the city is packed. Every morning, Teresa fights her way through the rush-hour traffic to catch the bus to school. Besides cars and buses, there are streetcars

to beware of, clanging past like trains on lines down the middle of the road. She enjoys school, especially English-language classes that started recently. But if she stays after school for sports, which she enjoys, she returns home during the evening rush hour.

Teresa is glad when Friday comes. She watches other families squeeze into their small Fiat cars and join the traffic jams on their way to the countryside for the weekend. She envies them a little for owning a country home, but at least she gets to enjoy Warsaw without the crowds. She and her mother do their shopping on Saturday morning. With bulging baskets, they stop for a cup of tea in a café on the Old Market Square. Teresa steals another look at the dress her mother bought her for a dance that evening. There were never clothes like that in the shops in the old days, her mother says. Teresa's new dress was expensive. She gives her mother a hug. In the afternoon, after her piano lesson, Teresa washes her hair, with an eye on the television screen because the local soccer team is playing.

On Sunday, Teresa wakes early and gazes out her high window. The streets are almost empty. She and her parents take a bus to the Old Town to attend Mass in the Church of the Holy Cross. The church is crowded as always. After that, they go for a walk in the Saxon Gardens. At noon, they pause beside the Tomb of the Unknown Soldier to watch the ceremonial changing of the guard. Then they go home for Sunday lunch of pork and sauerkraut, and a good book in the afternoon, before Teresa catches up on the last bits of homework for Monday.

## *MARRIAGE*

Poles have a deep respect for family. What could be more splendid than a wedding, that ceremony to mark the start of a new family? Celebration is obligatory. An invited guest might take three days off work to attend. Historically, a family that could not afford the cost of a wedding might sell a cow to pay for it.

In the old days, a landowner's permission might be needed for a peasant to marry—and he would be an honored guest at the festivities. Traditional rituals include the blessing of the bride and groom by the parents before the actual church ceremony; greenery on the bride's headdress representing her virginity; gates of greenery through which the couple pass on their way home from church; and the ceremonial greeting of the bride by her mother-in-law with bread and salt for her new home. Such customs are not always observed today, especially in the towns, where the bride wears a white gown and the groom a dark suit in Western style.

Poles traditionally believe that the success of a marriage will depend on the lavishness of the hospitality and the natural gaiety of the wedding feast. The band must not stop playing, so bridesmaids feed the musicians, while others pour sips of alcohol into their mouths!

In the evening, the couple are conducted to their bedroom to the sounds of a slow and solemn polonaise, danced to by the heads of the families and the married women. The following morning comes the "capping" of the new bride, the first wearing of the traditional headgear that shows she has joined the ranks of married people. By custom, the bride tries to put off that moment: she defends herself and throws off the cap; finally she agrees with much bitter sobbing, to show her reluctance to leave her family. This solemn ritual is no place for frivolous dancing or laughter.

The polonaise and "capping," like other traditional rituals, are seldom observed by modern couples in larger towns, but they are still practiced in the countryside.

## THE LAST DAYS

The family unit is important throughout life. There are few homes for the aged; the family looks after their aged relatives. Grandparents look after the grandchildren after school when the parents are working.

A girl visits a Jewish cemetery in Wroclaw. In Poland, people spend a lot of money on flowers to brighten graves and tombstones.

When there was a death in the family, relatives were required by tradition to wear black for a year. Nowadays a black mourning band suffices. A lot of money is spent on graves and tombstones. After the funeral, the wake is another good Polish party. There will be tribute speeches and toasts in spontaneous celebration of the departed's life.

# RELIGION

THE CATHOLIC FAITH is central to the life of the Polish people. They count their history as beginning when King Mieszko I was baptized and so adopted Christianity for Poland in A.D. 966. The oldest churches in the country preserve medieval Christian architecture. Six wooden churches in Malopolskie dating back to the Middle Ages are on the UNESCO World Heritage list.

Pope John Paul II is Polish, and it must please him immensely that his country probably has a higher proportion of Roman Catholics than any other country in Europe, excluding Vatican City itself. Around 95 percent of Poles profess Roman Catholicism.

## FIERCE CATHOLICS

Throughout history, Poland has been a fiercely defended outpost of Christian Europe. As Christianity spread through the Roman empire, differences of opinion arose between east and west. In A.D. 1054 the Orthodox Church broke ties with Rome. Russia aligned itself with the Orthodox movement, but Poland stayed firmly aligned with Rome.

Persecution can strengthen faith, and in the case of Poland, four decades of Communist-supported atheism failed completely. Instead, those years saw a religious revival, linked joyously with the election of a Polish pope. The Solidarity trade union was seen as an expression of the Christian values of cooperation and the dignity of work.

*Opposite:* **Mass in a church in Poland.**

*Below:* **Nuns are a common sight in Poland.**

## CHURCH AND LIFE

On Sundays, Polish Christians flood their churches, which may hold three or four services or Masses on Sundays to accommodate the congregations. On festival days, processions may block country roads for miles, carrying colorful banners with appeals to the Virgin Mary embroidered in gold and silver thread: "Holy Mary, Mother of God, protect us; do not abandon us, we are your children."

Lanes and road crossings in the countryside are lined with thousands of shrines, which are lovingly cared for and often adorned with ribbons and garlands. In winter, people trudge through the mud and snow, decorating shrines with twining boughs and paper flowers. If a shrine carries a cross, it commemorates a death. If it has a figure of the Madonna, it celebrates healing or a life saved. In most Polish homes there is an icon of the Virgin Mary or a portrait of Pope John Paul II, or both. The church is the heart of the village.

**A shrine decorated with flowers.**

Mass is a joyous gathering for Roman Catholics in Poland. Sunday is a holy day of obligation—and so are major Christian festivals. Fulfilling their religious obligation with enthusiasm is nothing strange for Poles. People can be found at prayer in almost every church. In 1966 Poland celebrated its 1,000th year as a Christian country.

Religion is not merely a comfort to older folk. Many young Poles are involved in the life of the church community. However, as is the case in most Western European nations, church attendance is falling among the under-30 crowd in Poland.

**TWO MODERN LEADERS**  In 1952 Cardinal Stefan Wyszynski, the primate of the Roman Catholic Church in Poland, was exiled to a monastery as part of the Communist attack on the Church. In 1956 the Polish party leader, Gomulka, freed Wyszynski because he needed his support. Wyszynski promptly demanded that the teaching of religion be reinstated in schools, that religious publications be restarted, and that imprisoned priests be released. All his demands were granted.

It was a strange partnership. The cardinal and the Communist were the only two leaders the Poles would trust. Wyszynski was not supporting the Communist regime; he was supporting national unity. Without Wyszynski, much of the Polish spirit would never have survived. His vital work continued through years of protest, right up to the formation of Solidarity.

Another Polish Church leader was Jerzy Popieluszko, who rose from humble beginnings as a farmer's son to became a fiery pro-Solidarity preacher. Father Popieluszko's outspoken comments during the days of martial law embarrassed the Communist state.

Despite being threatened and arrested by security forces, Father Popieluszko continued to speak out against the regime. On October 19, 1984, security forces kidnapped and murdered him. His driver escaped, so details of what had happened became known. The people were enraged and started riots. The government tried the murderers and sent the two ring-leaders to prison for 25 years.

Popieluszko's funeral became a Solidarity demonstration. His grave and the church he served, Saint Stanislaw Kostka, in northern Warsaw remain Solidarity shrines.

Poland's great cardinals Stefan Wyszynski (*left*) and Karol Wojtyla (later Pope John Paul II). When Cardinal Wyszynski visited Rome in 1957, he said, "In my Poland there is not enough room in the churches for the faithful."

*In Polish churches there are rows of lighted candles before an image of the Virgin Mary or of the church's patron saint. Worshipers often buy a candle in church as a form of almsgiving and leave it lit as a sign of their prayer.*

## POLAND'S FIRST POPE

When Karol Jozef Wojtyla appeared on the steps of Saint Peter's Basilica in Rome as Pope John Paul II, his first words were *"Non abbiate paura!"* ("Be not afraid!") It was 1978. Poland was in the grip of food shortages and price increases, strikes and arrests. The first non-Italian pope in more than 400 years and the first ever Polish pope, Wojtyla believed his election was some form of divine compensation for the sufferings of Poland.

Wojtyla was born on May 18, 1920, in Wadowice, about 20 miles (32 km) southwest of Krakow. He was baptized on June 20 the same year. His mother died when he was 9 years old; his older brother died when he was 12. His father became an admirable source of stability. Wojtyla recalls how seeing his father on his knees in prayer had a decisive influence on his early years. Sadly, his father died during the Nazi occupation. Before reaching age 21, Wojtyla had already lost the people he loved most.

When Wojtyla was at the Jagiellonian University in Krakow, the teachers were deported to concentration camps. He chose to train as a priest, which could be done only in the strictest secrecy. In order to stay in the area where college teaching was done in secret, Wojtyla worked in a stone quarry that supplied the sulfur factory in Krakow. Wojtyla became a priest, as his mother had hoped, and his career prospered. He eventually became the archbishop of Krakow and later a cardinal.

On October 16, 1978, Cardinal Wojtyla was elected Holy Father of the Roman Catholic Church, becoming Pope John Paul II. He was the pope of a Christian renewal—the first Slav pope.

**LIFE AS THE POPE** John Paul II wakes up at 5:45 A.M., not very easily, he admits. After meditating, he celebrates mass at 7 A.M. There may be a

short audience before breakfast with one or more guests. From 9 to 11 A.M. he is in his office, no visitors allowed. (In the old days in Krakow, he often locked himself in the chapel to write undisturbed.)

From 11 A.M. to 1:30 P.M., the pope receives visitors, then lunches with more guests. He may take half an hour's rest before going to the terrace to say his prayers. Then until 6:30 P.M., he works in his office with his assistants. Ministers and senior civil servants may try to interrupt him. Dinner, called supper in the Vatican, is at nearly 8 P.M. At 9 P.M. the pope retires to the chapel to pray. Often he goes to bed only after 11 P.M.

Pope John Paul II visited his homeland in 1979, 1983, and 1987, emphasizing that the Church, not Communism, truly ruled Poland. Millions traveled to see him and hear him preach, and there was a great surge of joy throughout the country. The happiness of a whole people could be read on their faces.

Poland post-Communism remains dear to the pope. He has made several pastoral visits to the country: in 1991, 1997, 1999, and 2002.

Pope John Paul II receives a big welcome in Krakow on one of his first papal visits to his homeland.

## THE BLACK MADONNA

The holiest shrine in Poland is the Jasna Gora, or Shining Mountain, the Pauline monastery at Czestochowa. The chapel of Jasna Gora houses the miraculous image of the Black Madonna, Poland's most treasured icon.

Legend has it that the image of the Black Madonna *(right)* was painted by Saint Luke on a tabletop made from dark cypress wood by Saint Joseph himself. The "black" quality of the image is merely the result of the aging of the pigments used. Rescued from the ruins of Jerusalem in A.D. 70, the icon was taken to Byzantium, presented to King Constantine, and in the 14th century presented to the Polish king Casimir, who put it in Czestochowa for safe keeping. Brigands once tried to steal the picture, but when they reached the German border, their horses, "moved by a miraculous force," refused to go any farther. So the picture was returned to the monastery.

Poles believe the real miracle took place about 350 years ago when a Swedish invasion swept over Poland but failed to capture the monastery. The monks, with a handful of Polish troops, held out until the Swedish commander called off the siege as his soldiers refused to go on fighting. They swore that "their own bullets came back at them, bouncing off the monastery walls." They said they saw a woman in a blue cloak floating above the shrine and covering the fortress with her mantle. They were convinced that heavenly forces were on the side of the monks. Perhaps even more miraculously, the shrine of the Black Madonna emerged safely from both Nazi and Communist occupations.

Every August, hundreds of thousands of pilgrims make the journey to Czestochowa—many entirely on foot, no matter where they start—and visit the high-domed Gothic chapel to kneel before the black-and-silver altar of the Virgin Mary. The chapel walls are hung with countless offerings in gratitude for healing miracles—silver plaques with a name and date, shaped like a heart, an eye, a limb, or even discarded crutches.

## SOME PLACES OF WORSHIP

Poland has more churches and priests today than before the war. There are many monasteries and about 30,000 nuns, many working in the community. In such a religious-minded nation, it is not surprising that there are some very impressive places of worship.

Most unusual must be the underground Chapel of the Blessed Kings hewn in crystal rock at the ancient salt mine of Wieliczka. Everything in the large ornate chapel is carved from salt: stairs, banisters, altar, and chandeliers. The acoustics are so good that the chapel is also used occasionally for concerts.

In Krakow is the Church of Saint Andrew, topped with twin baroque spires. The silver pulpit inside is a masterpiece in the shape of a ship manned by angelic mariners, as is the case in many Polish churches. Nuns attend services hidden behind a grille in the gallery.

On Silver Mountain (so called because of the silver bark of the birches) west of Krakow stands the church and hermitage of the Camaldolese monks at Bielany. Here lives a strict monastic order from Italy whose motto is *Memento mori* (Remember you must die). Monks live in seclusion, dressed in cream-colored robes, each with his own tiny cottage and vegetable garden that is his only source of food. They meet for common meals only five times a year. Except for times of prayer, they maintain a vow of silence. The white limestone church and the crypt (where bodies are sealed inside stone niches) may be visited by men, but women are only admitted once a year during major religious festivals.

*"Communism comes and goes, but the Catholic Church is here to remain."*

—*Cardinal Stefan Wyszynski*

**The Church of Saint Andrew in Krakow.**

## *THE CHURCH VERSUS COMMUNISM*

How can Catholics be Communists? They can't. The disciples of Lenin do not admit the existence of God. But a Communist would find it very difficult to ignore a religious holiday in Poland. They would be fully aware of the rejoicing and worship. Catholicism has been so deeply woven into Poland's national life that it is impossible for anyone living in Poland to escape it. Perhaps the Polish Church has played its part in bringing awareness of religion to those without it. Certainly, those Poles forced to pay lip service to the state were Catholics first and nominal Communists a distant second.

Although the Communists claimed that they practiced "religious toleration," the Church maintained that there was an official conspiracy to enforce atheism. The Church also vigorously defended the political rights of all Poles. Cardinal Wyszynski, the head of the Polish Church, and Karol Wojtyla, the archbishop of Krakow, preached that the government had to respect the people's right to participate in the political and social life of Poland.

The Church became a symbol of resistance against the system. The more the Polish people suffered, the more they found in religion an inexhaustible source of strength. That is why Communism lost its battle with the Church.

**A priest blesses religious articles that have been brought by worshipers.**

## *RELIGIOUS TOLERANCE*

Open-minded in most matters, Poles have a fairly narrow view when it comes to religion. A Protestant can be regarded as a foreigner. Yet Poland used to be famous for its religious tolerance. Those with unorthodox beliefs, whether Christian or not, found hospitality here.

It was to Poland that the oppressed Jews of Western Europe came for a haven, followed by the persecuted Bohemian Brotherhood (a Christian group formed in Bohemia in 1467). For several centuries, Poland had Europe's greatest concentration of Jews, secure in their own religious, cultural, and intellectual life. Today, you will still find places of worship for Protestants, Catholics, Jews, Muslims, and Buddhists. You will also see churches of the Eastern Orthodox creed with their double-barred, slanting crucifix.

Yet suspicion of those of a different faith is deep-rooted in Poland's history. In 1668 the Sejm declared that anybody who converted from Catholicism to another branch of Christianity would be exiled. Non-Catholics could not become Polish nobles—and thus members of the Sejm. Of course, not everybody obeyed such rules.

Poles today are free to worship as they please. Poland has perhaps a million non-Catholic believers, including an established Lutheran church. There are a small number of Methodists and Baptists, and a few thousand Muslim Tartars, but the Roman Catholic Church remains monolithic.

Political parties abound. Yet the suspicion of those who do not conform has been sadly strengthened by those very Communist years Poland is trying so hard to forget.

*The Communist asked, "Why is it, Father, that when you ring the bells for service all the villagers come running, but when I call a party meeting hardly anyone shows up?" The priest replied, "That's easy to answer. You and I both promise the people paradise, but you have already given them a taste of yours."*

*—an apocryphal story*

# LANGUAGE

POLISH IS A WESTERN SLAVIC LANGUAGE, along with Czech and Slovak. Russian, although written in the very different Cyrillic alphabet, is also a Slavic language, though it belongs to the East Slavic group. This double group of languages, often known as Balto-Slavic, is spoken by about 300 million people, more than half of whom speak Russian. As the Polish language differs slightly in different areas, the standard form of Polish is based on the dialect spoken in the Wielkopolskie region of western Poland. Not everyone in Poland speaks Polish at home. The Ukrainian and Belarusian minorities are bilingual. They speak Polish well, yet their home languages mark them as a separate language group.

## *LANGUAGE UNITES A NATION*

Polish uses the same alphabet as West European languages, with the exception of one letter and some accents (explained later). This was determined by the close association between Poland and the Roman Catholic Church and the use of Latin for worship and, therefore, writing. The earliest recorded use of Polish appears in 12th-century Church documents. There are many hymns, sermons, psalters, and law-court records dating from the early Middle Ages (14th and 15th centuries). Despite the fall of the Polish state in the late 18th century, Polish culture continued to develop. Language united the nation, yet local dialects reflecting former tribal patterns remain significant. For example, there are clearly recognized dialects known as Silesian, Great Polish, Little Polish, and Mazovian. Poles from Warsaw will find it hard to understand Poles from a village in the Tatra Mountains.

*Opposite:* **A man reads Poland's most widely read newspaper,** *Gazeta Wyborcza.*

*Below:* **An old lady looks on as a group of younger women engage in lively conversation.**

## SLAVS

No one quite knows how or where the Slav people originated. It is thought that, way back in prehistoric times, they settled in what is now western Russia and eastern Poland. Today, the majority of Poles, Czechs, and Slovaks are Slavs. Those who lived on the *po-more* (po-MO-zhe), or sea coast, were called Pomeranians, while those who lived in the *pole* (po-LE), or open country, were known as Polyanians. That could be where the name Poland comes from.

The original word Slav is said to come either from *slava* (sla-VA), meaning glory, or *slovo* (slo-VO), meaning speech. However, it was common in early medieval times for powerful mid-European nations to capture Slav children as servants. The word Slav (whether *sklave* in German, *slaaf* in Dutch, or *esclave* in French) then took on a new meaning—slave.

## *LANGUAGES IN EDUCATION*

There have been times in Polish history when it was forbidden to use Polish in schools and offices. Adam Mickiewicz, one of Poland's most admired poets, grew up in the 1820s, when the imperial Russian government was determined to eliminate the Polish language and all its cultural heritage. To succeed, a Pole was expected to learn Russian and convert to Russian Orthodoxy. Similarly, under Communist domination, Russian had to be taught in all schools from grade 5 to grade 12, and a course in Russian was compulsory in any university degree course.

For the Poles, their language has become more than just a means of communication; it is a symbol of the continued existence of the Polish nation. When the state tried to add new words and expressions to the Polish language, the Poles developed their own underground version of the language in which they could voice their hatred of Russian domination.

The third language offered for instruction in Communist-controlled Polish schools was French. But Poles today see no need for that either. They want to learn English, since it is a global language, and German, to build economic ties with their western neighbor. In fact, English is becoming seen as a sign of sophistication. Knowing English is a status symbol and helps career prospects. English teaching has become one of the most thriving businesses in Poland.

## EXPRESSIONS IN COMMON USE

If you hear a Pole saying "Jen Dobry," it is not someone's name, but a greeting, *"Dzien dobry!"* (jen DO-bri), which means "Good morning!" Before a drive, a Pole may wish you *"Szerokiej drogi!"* (she-ROK-yay DRO-gi), or "Have a wide road!"

A familiar form of address among friends and relations is *ty* (like the French *tu* or the German *du*). However, *ty* (ti) is not used when greeting older people or those in important positions, for whom the correct forms of address are *pan* (pan), or sir, and *pani* (pa-NEE), or madam. When addressing someone you know, it is impolite to use his or her surname. There is automatic respect for those with professional qualifications. For example, a doctor is called *panie doktorze* (pa-NYE dok-TO-zhe), or sir doctor.

Here are some common Polish expressions:

| | |
|---|---|
| *tak* (tahk) | yes |
| *nie* (nye) | no |
| *prosze* (PRO-she) | please |
| *dzienkuje* (jen-KOO-yeah) | thank you |
| *przepraszam* (pshe-PRASH-am) | sorry, or excuse me |
| *do widzenia* (do vid-ZEN-ia) | goodbye |

Some words you will recognize easily, such as auto, hotel, and stop. Many familiar greetings come from the strong religious element in Polish life. Villagers greet each other with "May Jesus Christ be praised," to which the response will be "Forever and ever." *Szczesc Boze* (shCHEshch BOH-zhe), meaning God bless you, is a common Polish goodbye.

*Glos Wielkopolski* is a Polish-language daily in Poznan.

## PRONUNCIATION

Knowing a few words in Polish goes a long way in making friends in Poland, so it is worth the trouble making sense of what may look like a jumble of consonants without vowels. The complexity of the Polish language goes back to the time when Poland disappeared from the map. Teachers were determined to save every detail of the old language. As a result, Polish did not really go through the same process that modernized and simplified so many European languages.

There are 32 letters and 45 sounds in the Polish language. The written form may look complicated, but the sounds each letter represents are at least consistent. The stress (beat) almost always falls on the next to last syllable. Three genders—masculine, feminine, neuter—create different cases and structures for some verbs, nouns, and adjectives. Nouns may change with a preceding preposition, so while the Polish word *miasto* (mya-STO) means town, it becomes *do miasta* (do mya-STA) if you want to say "to the town."

Polish vowels are pronounced as follows (the last three are unique to the Polish language):

a   as in "papa"

e   as in "ten"

i   as in "teeth"

ó   as in "coat"

u   as in "cuckoo"

y   as in "sit"

ą   nasalized, as with French *on*

ę   nasalized, as with French *un*

ó   the same as Polish *u*

There is also the diphthong *ie* (y-e), so that *nie wiem*, meaning "I don't know," sounds like "NY-e VY-em."

Consonants sound mostly the way they do in English, except for the following:

c   pronounced "ts" or "tz"

j   soft, like the "y" in "yes"

w   sounds like "v"

As in German, which is a neighboring language, some Polish consonants are softened when they come at the end of a word, so *b, d, g, w,* and *z* become *p, t, k, f,* and *s* respectively. The combination *ch* sounds guttural, as in the Scots word *loch*, and the accented ń goes wobbly, as in canyon or the Spanish *mañana*. The daunting combination *szcz* is easy to cope with if you remember the words "Polish chair," and use the "sh-ch" sound in the middle.

There is also a specially marked letter with a stroke across it: ł. This sounds like "w" and has the effect of making Władysław sound like "VWAH-DI-SWAV" and Łódz sound like WOOCH (ó with that accent sounds like "oo"). To pronounce the name of the founding leader of Solidarity, Lech Wałesa, say LE(ch) vaWENsa.

A Polish mailbox. The combination of consonants is unpronounceable for someone unfamiliar with Polish.

## *HANDS UP!*

Poles shake hands at every meeting, even with lifelong friends. A warm friendship gets an embrace as well. The older or more senior person will give the first greeting and expects a similarly courteous reply. A woman may hold out her hand for a man to kiss in greeting. "I kiss your hand," he says, in old-style courtesy. In the street, a man always walks on the left of the woman.

Europeans tend to use their hands freely as they talk (although the English tend to put their hands in their pockets). Poles gesticulate in much the same way as the French and Italians. Just occasionally, such sign language can be misunderstood. When Polish soldiers and airmen reached England during World War II, for example, they happily gave the V-sign for victory. Unfortunately, the Polish sign is the opposite of the British one (the back of the hand is shown), and some people thought they were being rude!

Like their fellow Europeans, Poles like to gesticulate with their hands as they talk.

There is a mildly rude gesture of defiance made by brandishing a fist while grabbing the inside of the elbow with the other hand. It is known as the Kozakiewicz gesture, in affectionate memory of the Polish pole-vaulter who was booed by the Russians at the 1980 Olympics in Moscow. Having made the jump that earned him the gold medal, he turned to the Russian crowd in full view of the television cameras and made this sign.

In rural areas, there are wooden crosses at many crossroads. Women coming to a junction will make the sign of the cross as a sign of faith.

Poles hold the fist with the thumb concealed as a good-luck gesture, indicating that "I'm holding thumbs for you." To show that they think someone is crazy, Poles do not circle a finger at their temple; they tap the middle of the forehead with the index finger.

# ARTS

ALTHOUGH THINGS ARTISTIC in Poland come originally from Slavic tradition (Eastern European and Russian), historical involvement with Western Europe has resulted in a mixture of artistic styles. Dominated geographically and politically by Russia and Germany, Poland has looked farther west to France for its cultural inspiration. It was in Paris that Frederic Chopin wrote most of his music and Marie Curie isolated radium.

## PART OF PRIDE AND PROTEST

When Poland was divided among its neighbors at the end of the 18th century, the arts bore the role of preserving the nation and its identity. Similarly, during the repressive four and a half decades of Communist control, protest against the state was voiced chiefly through theater and painting. Traditional costumes, dance, and decorative arts were kept alive in local regions, but the dull demands of industrialization led to their decline. Today, tourism has encouraged fresh artistic creativity, but on commercial terms, as the last generation of homegrown artists and artisans is dying out.

Specialities from particular regions include: glass paintings by the Zakopane mountain folk, the black pottery of Kielce, red sequined folk costumes from Krakow, multicolored cloth from Lowicz, the lacework of Koniakow, paper cutouts from Kurpie, and Silesian brass bands. The village of Zalipie is famous for the floral paintings that decorate its houses. It even has an annual competition of the best painted houses.

*Opposite:* **A Polish woman creates a traditional ornament from a ball and some string.**

*Below:* **A children's chair painted with a floral motif, a trademark of Polish handicraft.**

## A LAND OF MUSIC

The music scene is vibrant in Poland. Such names as Frederic Chopin, Ignace Jan Paderewski, and Artur Rubinstein are known worldwide. Poland has 10 symphony orchestras. International competitions, such as the Frederic Chopin piano competition and the Henryk Wieniawski violin competition, give added stimulus. Poland has 17 conservatories, over 100 music schools, almost 1,000 music centers, and many music societies and magazines. Warsaw stages opera and ballet performances, chamber concerts, and recitals every night, and regular performances by the national philharmonic orchestra. The city also plays host to the Jazz Jamboree, the oldest, most celebrated jazz festival in Eastern Europe.

But all that started with village musicians. Music based on the fiddle, pan pipes, or single-reed bagpipe (or in the Kurpie forest region, an accordion with a foot pump) created the dance rhythms of the mazurka and polka, which are still played in the traditional style in many villages, often for weddings and festivals. There is a folk festival each year at Kazimierz on the banks of the Vistula River that is very popular, attracting many young Poles to participate.

## FAMOUS MUSICIANS

**ARTUR RUBINSTEIN** (1887–1982) was a delightful, slightly old-fashioned showman—for many years, the world's best-loved concert pianist and well-known as an interpreter of the Romantic composers. He often performed Brahms, Schumann, and Chopin, and his recordings, made directly without correction,

A jazz club in Krakow. Jazz is popular in Poland.

unlike in modern recordings, remain dazzling. Born in Lodz, he made his professional debut at age 10 with the Berlin Philharmonic Orchestra. During World War II, Rubenstein, a Jew, moved to the United States. He became a U.S. citizen in 1946.

**WITOLD LUTOSLAWSKI** (1913–94), a Polish composer of the older generation compared to such up-and-coming composers as Penderecki, Krauze, and Gorecki, remains highly popular with concert-goers. His *Variations on a Theme of Paganini* was composed in 1941, during the Nazi occupation of Warsaw, when he was a café pianist and played duets with a friend after working hours. But he is best known for his stunning *Cello Concerto*, crammed with orchestral exuberance.

**FREDERIC CHOPIN** (1810–49) made his debut as a pianist at age 8. The son of a French father and a Polish mother, he made his home in Paris at age 21 and built a reputation for himself in fashionable salons as both composer and pianist.

Although he never lived in Poland again, Chopin continued to draw inspiration from his homeland, incorporating Slavic folk tunes and rhythms in his work. He revolutionized piano playing, concentrating on bravura solo pieces that show off the qualities of the instrument. His compositions for piano were characterized by an unusual lyrical and poetic quality. He died on October 17, 1849, and was buried in Paris.

Lutoslawski traveled widely as a conductor, performing his works with orchestras in Europe and the United States.

## LITERATURE

A bookstall overflowing
with books. Poles are avid
readers.

A bookstall overflowing with books. Poles are avid readers.

The earliest traces of Polish folklore and legend are preserved from medieval times. There exists, for example, the hymn chanted by King Jagiello's army before their victory over the Teutonic Knights at the Battle of Grunwald in 1410. Texts of Polish folk plays survive from the Renaissance.

The first public reference library on the European mainland was Bishop Zaluski's collection, which he donated to the Polish nation in 1747. The Sejm soon ordered printers to donate to the library the first copy of any book, and by the time the library was looted by the Russians in 1795, it contained over 500,000 volumes.

Writers are well-respected people in Poland. The 19th-century poet Adam Mickiewicz has the status of a national hero, and streets and squares are named after him. He wrote about Poland in a dark time and kept the flame of her spirit alive. His *Pan Tadeusz* and other works exerted a strong influence on future generations.

Polish-born prose writers have won the Nobel Prize in literature: Henryk Sienkiewicz for *Quo Vadis,* a story set in the time of Roman emperor Nero; Wladyslaw Reymont, whose epic novel of Poland, *Chlopi*, is strong with local color and historical detail; and Czeslaw Milosz and Wislawa Szymborka for their poetry. Joseph Conrad, the popular author of English seafaring novels such as *Lord Jim*, was actually Jozef Korzeniowski, born of Polish parents in Ukraine.

Although the Communist government imposed severe restrictions on writers, it encouraged books. In 1980, for instance, 11,315 different titles were published and 141.3 million books were printed, including 50 million fiction titles and 36.8 million school books. Today, the public libraries remain popular, and bookstalls spill onto sidewalks. It is a pity that the present economic climate forces booksellers to pay cash for any books they put into stock, because then most bookshops stock only what is guaranteed to sell—romances and thrillers by Wilbur Smith and Jeffrey Archer translated into Polish.

*"Poland drives out all its talented people. Frederic Chopin never saw this country again after the age of 20. He wrote all his great works abroad. Adam Mickiewicz wrote his* Pan Tadeusz *in exile. Marie (Curie) Sklodowska won her two Nobel Prizes in Paris not Poland."*

—James A. Michener
in Poland (1983)

## CZESLAW MILOSZ (1911–2004)

Polish writer Czeslaw Milosz delighted his country by winning the Nobel Prize in 1980 and subsequently returning home after 30 years in exile. His death was a deep loss for Poles. Born in 1911, half Polish, half Lithuanian, Milosz was educated in France but spent the war years in Poland, active in Warsaw's underground resistance movement. Hopeful of change, he joined the Polish diplomatic service. Disillusioned with the Communist regime, he went to teach Polish literature at the University of California.

A poet with a profound sense of vocation, he questions:

"I, who am I, a believer, dancing before the All-Holy?"

Then he answers his own question:

"A believer:

Though of weak faith, I believe in forces and powers

Who crowd every inch of the air …"

## THE POLISH PANORAMA

The most spectacular examples of Polish artwork include tiny figures carved from prehistoric amber and massive canvases depicting decisive moments in Polish history, such as Jan Matejko's *Battle of Grunwald* or the more intimate paintings of Jozef Simmler. Perhaps the greatest Polish painter is Jacek Malczewski (1854–1929), whose disturbing paintings concern Poland's "long period of darkness" in the 19th century. *Sunday in a Mine* shows a group of Polish dissidents sent to Siberia. Under the Communist regime, there was an insistence on "socialist realism"—photographic representations of heroic generals and bright-faced workers. Polish artists hated this and reacted by turning to abstract techniques. Victor Gorka and others expressed their individuality in obscure, suggestive vagueness. Freed from state censorship, Polish art is exploring new themes. Marian Kruczek, for example, makes insect-like sculptures from scrap steel and plaster.

## CINEMA

Despite tight state control and extreme censorship during Communism, Polish cinema produced some of the greatest films and filmmakers of the late 20th

Intricate Polish handicrafts displayed on the streets of Warsaw's Old Town Square.

century. Poland's first film company, Sphinx, was launched in 1909 and thrived in the inter-war period. After World War II, Polish film had a series of international hits by such directors as Andrzej Munk and Andrzej Wajda, who in 2000 received a lifetime-achievement award from the Academy of Motion Picture Arts and Sciences.

These and a few other filmmakers founded what became known as the Polish school of filmmaking. Oscar winner Roman Polanski, super successful in both Europe and Hollywood, continues to make films such as *The Pianist* (the moving biography of Wladyslaw Szpilman) and an adaptation of Charles Dickens's *Oliver Twist*. Jerzy Skolimowski, also well-regarded in Europe and the United States, cowrote Polanski's first feature film, *Knife in the Water*. Skolimowski has also won important prizes for his own movies, including *Walkover*, *Barrier*, and *Start*.

Another influential Polish filmmaker was Krzysztof Kieslowksi. Considered by many to have articulated the soul of central Europe, his masterwork is *The Decalogue*, 10 films loosely based on the Ten Commandments. Individually, the films can seem enigmatic and not following standard American storytelling norms, but as a whole they articulate difficult and delicate moral issues faced by people living in a post-industrial world. Kieslowski died in 1996.

These filmmakers studied at the National Higher School of Film, Television, and Theater in Lodz. The school also produced some of the most influential cinematographers, such as Pawel Edelman, Slawomir Idziak, and Edward Klosinski.

*One of the earliest movie cameras was made by a Pole, Piotr Lebiedzinski, in 1893.*

## *THEATER*

Live theater has always been welcomed in Poland. English traveling players used to visit there. German translations of Shakespeare's plays were performed in Gdansk even during Shakespeare's lifetime. After the downfall of the Polish state, theater played an enormous role in preserving the Polish language and spirit. Drama was often used as a medium of political protest.

During the 1960s, the Polish Laboratory Theater (the Theater of 13 Rows) in Wroclaw gained an international reputation for its experimental work. Under director Jerzy Grotowski, it toured Western Europe and the United States, and was acclaimed an important new direction in theater. In January 1968, the Communist authorities banned as anti-Russian a production of *Forefather's Eve*, a play by the poet Adam Mickiewicz. Poles revered his work and protested violently.

Social comment is made on both sides of the footlights, for audiences are encouraged to respond vigorously. Irony and satire are strong elements in Polish theater. Working now in the United States, Polish playwright Janusz Glowacki uses shrewd observations on life in Com-

## MUSHROOM SATIRE

In the 1960s, a popular act from the Student Satirical Theater in Warsaw featured a middle-aged man with a basket of mushrooms meeting a young man. It is clear that the older man has been in the forest since September 1939. He becomes increasingly disturbed to hear what has been happening in Poland since then. "Don't worry. It's all right," the young man assures him. But the mushroom gatherer grabs his basket and heads back into the forest and into the past. "Wait a minute," says the young man. "I'm coming with you." He winks at the audience. "I have to convince him," he adds.

munist Eastern Europe to entertain theatergoers in the United States. In *Antigone in New York*, a Polish thief and a Russian drunk are homeless New Yorkers determined to show their defiance of "the authorities."

There are three drama schools in Poland, and admission is very competitive. Poles flock to live entertainment at the country's 91 theaters (including 24 puppet theaters), 19 opera and musical theaters, and 21 concert halls. Warsaw's Grand Theater houses an impressive Theater Museum.

## THE MASS MEDIA

There has been a media explosion in Poland. Many people have more than 10 Polish-language television stations to choose from. Also popular are foreign-language stations. Many Poles have satellite hookups and can watch programs from around the world.

Television is the most controlled medium in Poland. It remains largely in the hands of the government and is still sometimes used as a propaganda tool. Imported movies and programs are televised, often dubbed in Polish, with the original soundtrack audible in the background. This makes listening a chore. Video and DVD rental shops do good business, however.

There are more than 10 national newspapers and magazines, all privately owned and free of government interference. Growing in popularity is the Internet, which can be accessed by all and controlled by none. There is even a BBC Polish-language site.

**A Polish theater.**

## FROM AUSTERE TO ORNATE

A street corner decoration. Old Polish buildings are often decorated with lavish detail.

In a country that has so often been fought over, invaded, destroyed, and rebuilt, one would expect a variety of architectural styles. There are stern Romanesque churches, spired and fluted late-Gothic cathedrals, warm brick town halls, and ornate masterpieces of the Italian Renaissance and Baroque periods. Poles of the 16th and 17th centuries admired the beauty of Islamic art, which complemented the popular Baroque architecture. Eastern textiles replaced Flemish tapestries on the walls of manor houses. Onion-shaped turrets topped circular towers in the style of minarets.

The Poles themselves live comfortably amid the confusion of gaunt "socialist realism" and decorative historical relics. They are more aware than the average tourist of just how many buildings that look historical are really clever reconstructions, especially in Warsaw. The Baroque Church of the Holy Cross in the capital city was completely rebuilt from paintings and old photographs after the city was destroyed in 1945. It is topped by a gigantic statue of Jesus Christ that was brought triumphantly back from Germany where it had been destined for scrap.

Many old houses such as those in the Old Town Square in Warsaw or most of Krakow have painted facades that often imitate carved classical styles. The same *trompe l'oeil* (eye-tricking) painting was used inside many of the sumptuous palaces as well as those now being restored in Wilanow Palace in Warsaw. Yet

## WITNESSES OF HISTORY

Castles and palaces such as Wilanow Palace (*right*) are undoubtedly jewels in the Polish architectural crown. Wawel Castle in Krakow is the most impressive. Built on a rocky embankment overlooking the Vistula River, its red-brick foundations, cream walls, and dark slate roofs mix Romanesque, Gothic, and Renaissance styles,  and its ornate reception rooms recall ages of elegance long past. Wawel is the first stop along the popular Eagle Nest Trail, a chain of medieval castles built by King Casimir the Great in the 14th century, which ends at the Royal Castle of Warsaw.

perhaps even more breathtaking is the gilt-and-marble Baroque decoration in the bigger churches.

Although the city cathedrals and castles are undoubtedly impressive, it is the village houses that show the genuine Poland most clearly—red brick and tile, steep sloping roofs against the winter snow, and always the spire of the village church.

In Pomerania, houses are wide but low, as if ducking down to avoid the wind. In Masuria, they are smaller and sometimes thatched. In the mountains, houses are made of wood and have a pointed roof. The unsightly new square cottages with flat roofs that are seen almost everywhere are made of mass-produced building blocks. A recent development is the open-air museum, or *skansen* (SCAN-sen), which gathers models of traditional rural architecture to preserve the actual buildings. Wooden churches, mills, houses, and barns are equipped and decorated according to the style of the period. The country's oldest *skansen*, in Wdzydze Kiszewskie, Pomorskie, was founded in 1906.

# LEISURE

SPORTS DOMINATES Polish television. The achievements of Polish athletes definitely get full coverage. When Wojtek Fibak made his mark on world tennis, for example, his matches were televised in Poland. As a result of the general enthusiasm, tennis courts were built in country districts, and the sport is now far more popular than it ever was.

## MODERN SPORTS

For many years, there was a great emphasis on school sports, and some lucky children were sent to special schools as well for extra training. But school sports are declining as there is no longer money for equipment. There are some private sports clubs, but these are expensive and only wealthier parents can afford the membership fees. Swimming remains popular, as does "artistic gymnastics" and synchronized swimming. Hockey, ice-hockey, volleyball, and soccer are all popular.

Some boys attend soccer practice for perhaps an hour after school, three times a week. Others play basketball or volleyball in the park. Yet others play "streetball," which is like basketball but with few players on each side (three, for example) and only one basket.

On Saturday mornings, people may close off part of a street and set up goalposts for soccer matches. Prizes may be donated by a sportswear manufacturer. Rain or shine, the matches are played through to a much-cheered finale. Soccer is the top spectator sport in Poland.

Motorcycle racing is increasing in popularity. Large crowds turn up at local club meetings. Several Polish riders have already taken part in international events.

Many Poles jog for sport and take part in local fun runs and serious marathons. There is a sports stadium in most towns.

*Opposite:* **A couple enjoys quiet conversation at a café in Krakow.**

Hunters get ready for hunting season, which opens in early November with the fox chase, or Hubertus Run, named after Saint Hubertus, the patron of hunters.

## TRADITIONAL SPORTS

The Poles have a traditional love of the outdoor life. They have loved horses for centuries. With a history full of wild cavalry charges, it is no surprise how many riding stables and stud farms there are in Poland. Poland has a long tradition of breeding Arabian horses, particularly at Janow Podlaski, close to the frontier with Russia. Horse-riding, though obviously not a cheap pastime, remains popular. Hunting and fishing are carefully controlled with permit requirements.

Older Poles especially love rifle shooting. Almost every large town has its marksmen's society. But nowhere is there as colorful a tradition as the Brotherhood of the Cock in Krakow. The brotherhood parades through the city in traditional finery before going to the military firing range for the shoot-off with target rifles. This ritual dates back to when all citizens were expected to practice fighting skills, whether with bow, sword, or musket. A shooting competition evolved, with a wooden cock set on a high pole as the target. The one to shoot off the last remaining splinter became Cock King for a year and paid no municipal taxes!

## SOCCER

This is the game that all small boys play in the streets and all fathers cheer on weekends. Poland has three soccer leagues: the first and second are national, the third provincial. Many teams are named after factories that sponsor them. A leading club is Hutnik Warsaw, which in 1992 signed a Russian player in exchange for a television set and a video recorder. There was a general lack of hard cash. Another Warsaw team bought a Russian player for a truckload of potatoes! Legia Warsaw won the 1993 club championship, beating LKS Lodz on goal average. The soccer season runs from March to November. Winter is too cold, so the June-July vacation, known as the cucumber season, is time for a rest, soccer training camps, and friendly international games.

Poland takes part regularly in international soccer tournaments and won the silver medal in the 1992 Barcelona Olympics. The following year, having drawn their home match in the World Cup against England, Polish soccer players were amused to note that the English, who invented the game, then lost their own match against the United States.

## POLAND'S OLYMPIC RECORD

Poland was slow in building up to an Olympic sporting standard until the years after World War II. The leap to 21 medals in 1960 shows the emphasis placed on sports and training by the Communist regime.

After 62 nations, including the United States, boycotted the 1980 Olympics in Moscow because of the Soviet invasion of Afghanistan, the Soviet Union in turn boycotted the 1984 Olympics in Los Angeles. Most Communist countries, including Poland, had to follow suit.

Polish male gold-medal athletes have included Jozef Schmidt (triple jump in 1960 and 1964), Jacek Wszola (high jump in 1976), Tadeusz Slusarski and Wladyslaw Kozakiewicz (pole vault in 1976 and 1980), and Bronislaw Malinowski (3,000-m steeplechase in 1980). Among the female winners were Irena Szewinska (400-m relay in 1964 and 200 m in 1968) and Otylia Jedrzejczak (200-m butterfly in 2004). Poland also boasts eight gold-medal boxers.

In the 1992 Olympics, Poland's total of 19 medals put the country in 14th position among 64 medal-winning countries. Poland's prowess in boating won them three medals in the kayak events.

In the Winter Olympics, held since 1924, Poland ranks 19 among 25, with a total of only four medals.

*Poland's Olympic gold, silver, and bronze wins:*

| | G | S | B |
|---|---|---|---|
| 1924 | 0 | 1 | 1 |
| 1928 | 1 | 1 | 3 |
| 1932 | 2 | 1 | 4 |
| 1936 | 0 | 3 | 3 |
| 1948 | 0 | 0 | 1 |
| 1952 | 1 | 2 | 1 |
| 1956 | 1 | 4 | 4 |
| 1960 | 4 | 6 | 11 |
| 1964 | 7 | 6 | 10 |
| 1968 | 5 | 2 | 11 |
| 1972 | 7 | 5 | 9 |
| 1976 | 7 | 6 | 13 |
| 1980 | 3 | 14 | 15 |
| 1988 | 2 | 5 | 9 |
| 1992 | 3 | 6 | 10 |
| 1996 | 7 | 5 | 5 |
| 2000 | 6 | 5 | 3 |
| 2004 | 3 | 2 | 5 |

## WINTER SPORTS

Skiing is Poland's most popular winter sport. Not even the dreariness of the Communist regime could weaken the country's enthusiasm. When winter comes, Poles make an overnight train journey to the High Tatras, waking up to the sight of snowcapped mountains and spruce forests. The Tatra range has lakes, waterfalls, hidden valleys, and a wealth of old legends. Its people are reserved and ceremonially courteous.

The picturesque Zakopane ski resort is the winter sports capital of Poland. Its name means buried. Zakopane has hosted the International Ski Championship and the Olympic Winter Games. Its two ski jumps are among the best in Europe. There is a cable-car station near the Kasprowy Wierch, a peak 6,450 feet (1,985 m) high. In a good winter, as many as 50 ski lifts are in operation. For Poles, this is not a fashion show or a demonstration of skill. It is an adventure, with simple accommodation, good company, and perhaps a glass of something warming by the log fire afterward.

*"When life gets unbearable, there is always Zakopane."*

*—Polish saying*

## WHAT TO DO

Public entertainment is expanding. Most towns have a cinema, though almost all the movies come from the United States. Warsaw's official website lists 26 movie theaters, 40 theaters and concert halls, 35 museums, 27 libraries, and 21 galleries. Warsaw, Lodz, Krakow, and Poznan are some of the cities with quality theaters and opera houses. Theaters, museums, and everything else close on Monday.

Three terrestrial channels, and cable and satellite television give Poles a choice of 40 channels altogether. Poles often prefer just putting on some music. Music permeates Polish culture. From classical to popular, it is nearly everywhere. American pop is popular.

The Grand Theater in Teatralny Square in Warsaw.

## WHERE TO GO

Even Poles are starting to be tourists inside their own country. Freed from state restrictions and aided by improved transportation, they are trying out more than the traditional winter sports.

Poland has nearly 1,000 youth hostels, more than any other country. Conditions are often spartan. Many are former school buildings in which the desks have been replaced by beds.

However, there is a full range of hotels, and many large firms retain holiday apartments that are allocated to deserving employees. The universal outdoor activity, and probably the cheapest, is hiking. Trails are well marked and, in the mountains, spectacular.

# FESTIVALS

THE ANCIENT ANNUAL CYCLE of ordained church fasts and festivals remains the pattern of the year for Poles. Advent anticipates the coming of Christmas, which celebrates the birth of Jesus Christ. Ash Wednesday marks the start of Lent, a period of fasting that recalls Jesus's own fast in the wilderness. Palm Sunday welcomes Holy Week, which climaxes on Good Friday and Easter Sunday.

Other important festivals are scattered through the year, with a regular celebration on Sundays.

## HARVEST FESTIVAL

Although now recognized as the time to visit the fields and orchards to thank God for the year's harvest, the harvest traditions are far older than Christianity. Old pagan rituals were steadily curtailed during the Middle Ages, but one that survives is that of the *koza*, or goat. A boy with a sheepskin over his head and shoulders and accompanied by carol singers goes visiting to bring prosperity, help the growth of the corn, and assure a successful harvest.

*Above:* **Dancers at a folk festival.**

*Opposite:* **Sports events are also occasion for celebration. Here, Polish fans wave flags under the fireworks display at the opening ceremony of the Ski Jumping World Cup in Zakopane in 2004.**

At the harvest home celebrations at the season's end, girls carry the harvest wreath, made of corn and topped with the figure of a cock or a girl. When the girls finish their special dance, they are supposed to give the wreath to the farmer, and the next year's sowing will start with seed crumbled from the wreath, which is made of last year's crop.

A typical harvest procession today is led by a cross, flanked by choir boys in cassocks and lacy surplices, and followed by the congregation. The procession will visit the fields and barns to thank God for His goodness and ask for His continued bounty.

## *HOLY WEEK*

After the self-imposed disciplines of Lent, the week preceding Easter is a period of varied festivities. Holy Week in Poland is heralded by spring fairs, selling early-grown vegetables and livestock.

These lead into Palm Sunday, a fine reason for the processions Poles love. The palms may be small sprays of everlasting flowers or willow branches mixed with white catkins. In the mountain villages, men make palms up to 15 feet (4.6 m) in height, adorned with flowers, ribbons, and colored papers.

On Maundy Thursday, there may be scenes similar to England's Guy Fawkes bonfires. Some Polish communities take symbolic revenge on Judas Iscariot, hanging a stuffed figure of him, dragging it outside the village, and there burning it or throwing it into the river.

Good Friday is celebrated with solemn services, and then perhaps a visit to a specially created life-size portrayal of the Holy Sepulchre. In Rzeszow, this has become mixed up, in local tradition, with King Jan III Sobieski's victory at the battle of Vienna, so there are Turkish soldiers on guard outside the tomb. Good Friday is a holy day, not a holiday. Some families fast all day.

In Kalwaria Zebrzydowska near Krakow, a spectacular passion play tells the story of Jesus Christ's passion. The play is as popular locally as the Oberammergau cycle is in Bavaria. The main roles of the play are performed by local priests, while pilgrims play the disciples, Pharisees, and soldiers. They consider this a great honor. Followed by thousands of devout spectators, the play visits over 20 chapels that represent the Stations of the Cross—the highlights of Jesus Christ's passion.

On Holy Saturday, homemakers do their Easter baking, and children take baskets of eggs to church to be blessed.

## WET MONDAY

On Easter Monday, the custom of Smigus-Dyngus (water-dousing) provides some light relief. Gangs of children arm themselves with water guns or with buckets and sprays, and roam the streets in search of victims. The boys chase the girls. They might use just a spray of perfume or a plastic lemon as a water gun or a bucket of water. The first one up in the morning is supposed to

have the right to spray others, who are not supposed to fight back. (They usually do!)

This custom originated from ritual washing, a purification intended to bring rain to fields sown with grain. Today it is thought of as a damp piece of good luck!

## *EASTER*

The main event of the Catholic year, Easter attracts larger-than-usual crowds to church. The Paschal Lamb, not the Easter bunny, is the focus. Cakes are decorated with a lamb, made either of sugar or wood. The traditional Easter cake is *mazurek* (ma-ZUR-ek), a thin layer of shortbread pastry with different iced flavors, such as chocolate, coffee, and caramel.

Polish children enjoy Easter eggs as much as other children in the world. Eggs are hardboiled and decorated. They are eaten at the Easter breakfast, after Mass. The old way was to boil them with onion skins to dye them a rich brown. In western Poland, the eggs are stained in a single color; this may be red, yellow, or green. Around Krakow and the south, many colors are used, sometimes with red cutout stencils. In Mazowsze, people cover the eggs with very fine linen, ornamented with the pith from bulrushes.

# HIGH DAYS AND HOLY DAYS

On holy days of obligation, Catholics are expected to attend Mass and avoid all unnecessary work. Sunday is a holy day of obligation. There are also 10 special days that the Poles call High Days: Christmas, the Circumcision, the Epiphany, the Ascension, Corpus Christi, the Assumption, Saints Peter and Paul Day, All Saints' Day, the Immaculate Conception, and Saint Joseph's Day.

The feast of Corpus Christi honors what is referred to as the real presence of Jesus Christ in the Eucharist, the consecrated bread distributed to Catholics during Mass. Corpus Christi is observed with colorful processions on the Thursday after Trinity Sunday, with the Corpus Christi, the consecrated bread, held high with great reverence and rejoicing.

**Church of Saints Peter and Paul. The feast day of these two apostles is a holy day of obligation when Catholics have to attend Mass.**

Lent, the 40 days before Easter, is a time of fasting, when fat, butter, and eggs are forbidden. So on Shrove Tuesday, the day before Lent begins, all these ingredients have to be used up. Pancakes seem an obvious way. In Europe this day is known as *Mardi Gras* (Fat Tuesday), when people not only feast but enjoy colorful carnivals.

The first day of Lent is Ash Wednesday. During Mass, ashes from the previous year's palms are put in a bowl and sprinkled with holy water. The priest dabs his thumb in the ash and marks a cross on the forehead of each worshiper as a sign of penance.

Lady Day is the traditional name for the Feast of the Annunciation, celebrated on March 25. It recalls how the Archangel Gabriel told Mary of the forthcoming birth of Jesus.

## THE LEGEND OF THE CHRISTMAS SPIDERS

This tale came to Poland from Germany. When Jesus was a boy, so the legend goes, he came to a poor farmhouse on Christmas Eve. The front door was closed. Outside in the cold, he found a family of spiders. They were crying, for they had seen the Christmas tree in the house, bare and without decoration because the family could not afford such luxuries.

So the boy Jesus opened the door and let the spiders in. They hurried across the floor and swarmed all over the tree. When they had finished, its branches were festooned with their sticky grey cobwebs.

Jesus knew that the farmer's wife kept her house spotlessly clean and had no love of cobwebs. So he blessed the tree, and the grey threads turned to strands of silver and gold. And that is why Christmas trees have shining, glistening strands of tinsel.

## *WE WISH YOU A MERRY CHRISTMAS*

In the old tradition, a small, sweet-smelling spruce tree known as the *podlaznik* (pod-LAZ-neek) is hung from the rafters on Christmas Eve and decorated with apples, cookies, walnuts wrapped in shiny paper, and star-shaped paper cutouts. Some put their Christmas tree more conventionally on the floor. Young men go from house to house calling Christmas greetings, and if one of them catches a young woman under the hanging *podlaznik*, he is allowed to kiss her.

Christmas Eve is more important than Christmas Day in Polish culture. The eve begins when the first star is sighted. People put on their best clothes, then look for their presents under the Christmas tree. A special supper starts with the sharing of bread—the father first, then his family. The meal may consist of fish, noodles, wild mushrooms, cabbage, or herring, but no meat. Alcohol is also not served, because the family will go to the midnight Mass.

On the morning of Christmas Day, the family may go to Mass again. Then comes lunch, with *rosol*, a clear chicken and macaroni soup, and all kinds of cold meats: ham, salami, horseradish, potatoes, and salad.

The creche, or *szopka* (SHOP-ka), traditionally consists of puppets or wooden figures representing Herod, the Devil, Death, and the Holy Family in a scene of adoration. A *szopka* competition is held every year on the Main Market Square in Krakow.

**Girls in traditional white and boys in their best suits celebrate First Holy Communion at the Jasna Gora monastery.**

## *FAMILY OCCASIONS*

The big family occasions are baptism, first communion, and marriage. Nearly all Poles receive communion for the first time when they are

children. This is a very important event for the whole family, and relations come from all over the country to attend. The children will wear new clothes, often in traditional style.

Wedding anniversaries are carefully noted, because the family unit is very important in Poland. An extra big party is held every 10 years.

Mother's Day is also very important. Children may perform a play in school and invite their parents.

As in many Catholic countries, your birthday is celebrated not on your biological birthday but on your Name Day, the feast day of the saint you are named after.

But Poles don't need an excuse for a party. One father, a twinkle in his eye, explains, "If my boy comes home with a good note from his teacher, then we celebrate. If he comes home without a good note, then the teacher must have forgotten to give it to him, so we celebrate anyway!"

## THE ANNUAL PLEDGE

The Blessed Virgin Mary is the patron of the Polish Crown. Poland's knights used to ride into battle singing *Bogurodzica* (Mother of God). When the Swedish troops were driven out of the country, the King of Poland pledged himself and his nation to the service of "Our Lady, Queen of the Crown of Poland."

To this day, Polish Catholics renew their vows to the Blessed Virgin Mary every year, traditionally at the shrine of the Black Madonna at Czestochowa.

*"Every day is good for celebration!"*

—*Polish saying*

### PUBLIC HOLIDAYS

These are the official public holidays in Poland:

| | | | |
|---|---|---|---|
| January 1 | New Year's Day | November 1 | All Saints' Day |
| March/April | Good Friday | November 11 | National Independence Day |
| | Easter Monday | December 25, 26 | Christmas |
| May 1 | Workers' Day | | |
| May 3 | Constitution Day | | |
| May/June | Corpus Christi | | |

**WORKERS' DAY** was, during the years of Communist control in Poland, an annual reminder of the power of Moscow. But on May 1, 1984, Lech Walesa and other Solidarity workers managed to join the state-organized May Day parade, flashing V-for-victory signs as they passed the government officials on the reviewing stand. On May Day in 1988, protests urged by Solidarity took place in 12 cities. This holiday is not celebrated as festively as it once was.

**CONSTITUTION DAY** is the anniversary of the adoption in 1791 of the Polish constitution, the first in Europe and the second in the world. Celebrated with great fanfare in Polish communities outside Poland, it is a subdued day of official ceremonies inside the country.

# FOOD

THE GUIDING PRINCIPLE OF POLISH CUISINE is to reach the heart through the stomach. As a rule, Poles eat simply but fully. Most cannot afford to eat out often, but when they do, they make the most of it. Restaurants stay open through the day.

Breakfast is usually eaten at around 7 A.M. and is little more than a sandwich with tea or coffee. A second breakfast often follows before midday. This is a light lunch, perhaps including fried eggs and ham or frankfurters, or a plate of cold meats, cheese, rolls, and jam. The main hot meal comes in the late afternoon, and there may be a snack of cold meats or cheese with bread at night. The biggest meal of the week is Sunday lunch. That goes on a long time!

*Opposite:* **A covered market in Wroclaw.**

*Below:* **A shop window displays bread, cheese, and fruit—all you need for a simple Polish meal.**

## *BREAD AND CAKES*

In Communist times, most of the bread was mass-produced, rather hard, made of rye and often flavored with caraway seeds. Today, more and more private bakeries are providing fancy loaves, croissants, and other breads, as well as the still popular rye. There is a darker brown bread flavored with honey and a white sour rye bread that is good with cheese. Bread is only served in a restaurant if ordered, but Poles eat a lot of bread at home, with butter or margarine, and various kinds of jam, such as plum, strawberry, or blackberry.

Cakes are a favorite. Even small villages have their own cake shop. *Sernik* (sir-NEEK), or cheesecake, is popular everywhere, and you may also be treated to poppy-seed cake, sponge cake topped with plums, or

Signs advertise hamburgers, pizzas, and *flaki,* a very popular tripe dish.

marble cake. Festive occasions call for special cakes. Wedding cakes are ring-shaped and studded with round, hard biscuits and decorations made of sweetened dough. Traditionally, small animal-shaped cakes were thrown at the bridal couple as they returned from the wedding ceremony, and two oblong-shaped cakes, baked together, were given to the couple at their first breakfast as husband and wife. For baptisms, cakes are baked 4 feet (1.2 m) long in the belief that the size of the cake will determine the child's happiness and good luck. For funerals, there are special rolls and cakes called *kolaczki* (ko-LACH-kee). Flat pancakes, or *placnik* (platz-NEEK), are made for All Souls' Day, while Easter cakes are flavored with chocolate, coconut, cream, and poppy seeds.

## MEAT EATERS

In spite of economic shortages, Poles have remained insatiable meat eaters. Beef and pork are their favorites, with hams and different types of sausages for snacks during the day. The most common meat dish is a fried pork cutlet served in a thick sauce. Because meat is expensive, the average Polish family serves it mostly on feast days or to visitors. Otherwise the menu is vegetable-based and mostly boiled. One favorite meat is Krakow sausage, a special round, brown, very dry sausage, a

## IT CAN'T BE BEETEN!

Beets are a many-purpose vegetable, a mainstay for the Polish cook. They can be served hot or cold, made into soup or pickled. They are rich in potassium, calcium, and vitamin A.

Beetroot soups include the famous *barszcz* (BARshch), or borscht, as known to Americans, a clear, spicy red soup served with a small meat pastry, such as a sausage roll. *Botwinka* (bot-VEEN-ka) is made from the leaves of baby beetroot and served with a hard-boiled egg.

*Chlodnik* (hwod-NEEK) is a cold pink Lithuanian soup with sour milk and crunchy strips of onion or green vegetables. It looks a little like a strawberry milkshake. Only young beetroot, both bulb and stem, are used to make *chlodnik*.

Salads are also made from beetroot and horseradish. Every Polish vegetable garden will have a few rows of beetroot for the home larder.

delicacy with dark rye Polish bread and with beer. Other national dishes are *golabki* (go-WOM-bkee), cabbage leaves stuffed with minced meat and rice; *bigos* (BEE-goss), sauerkraut with spicy meat and mushrooms; *flaki* (fla-KEE), tripe served boiled or fried with carrots and onions; and *golonka* (gol-ON-ka), pig's leg with horseradish and pease pudding.

Vegetables are usually boiled or mashed potatoes, though there are french fries for tourists, and cabbage, boiled or pickled as sauerkraut. Salads tend to be unimaginative. Sliced tomatoes and onions, or plain lettuce are more common than cucumber in cream, grated beetroot, or wild forest mushrooms.

The foundation of Polish cuisine is old Slavic cooking. The Slavs used both sweet and sour cream to make their soups and gravies smooth and piquant as is done in Russian cooking. The widespread use of smoked bacon was typical in what was the East Prussian area of Poland where it was considered almost a sin if a housewife did not fry mashed potatoes in bacon fat until brown, or if she included them in a pot of dumplings. The flavor of smoked bacon and the tartness of sour cream are often blended together in festive veal or beef roasts browned in bacon fat and sauced with cream.

Poles like pickled herring, with onions or in sour cream, particularly between glasses of vodka. In the coastal and mountain areas, people may also eat carp or trout, usually grilled whole to a crispy brown.

## EATING OUT

A Polish street vendor sells grilled sausages.

There is a wide selection of eating places in Poland. Quality once varied from day to day depending on the supply of ingredients, but that is no longer a problem. Most expensive hotels and restaurants offer consistently high-quality dining. These are open from late morning to mid-evening. Some do not open until 1 P.M., as alcohol may not be sold before that time.

Cafés are a way of life. They range from cheap soup kitchens, where people munch on grey bread sandwiches and drink bottles of very pungent beer, to hotdog stalls, Western-style fast-food outlets, and milk bars, which are often stocked with delicious pastries and ice creams. All the big cities offer a wide range of culinary experiences—from Chinese to vegetarian specialities, and from fast food (such as McDonald's and KFC) to high-priced world-class cuisine.

## WARMING SOUPS

Polish cuisine is geared to a cold, damp climate. There is a heavy emphasis on soups and meat, especially pork, as well as freshwater fish. Cream is used a lot, and pastries are often rich and delectable.

## BIGOS

If there is a Polish national dish, it might well be *bigos*, a long-established favorite of sauerkraut, cabbage, mushrooms, onions, and a variety of meats—originally game but now mostly pork and sausage. *Bigos* is eaten with mustard or very hot horseradish, but never chutney. It is a seasonal dish, as it relies on the supply of sauerkraut, the pickled cabbage made usually at summer's end to last through winter. This recipe for *bigos* is for six people, but if you cannot get the sauerkraut and dried mushrooms, it won't taste Polish at all!

1½ ounces (42.5 g) dried mushrooms
2 pounds (907 g) fresh sauerkraut
9 ounces (255 g) cabbage, cut finely into strips
9 ounces (255 g) each of pork, beef, and sliced smoked sausage
1 teaspoon vegetable oil
5 ounces (142 g) chopped onions
5 pimentos
4 bay leaves
1 clove of garlic
Salt and pepper
A little tomato paste

Soak the mushrooms in water. Boil the sauerkraut and fresh cabbage separately until tender. Cut the pork and beef into cubes. Fry in oil with the onions. Cook the mushrooms in boiling water. Leave to cool, then chop finely. Put everything into a large casserole dish with the seasonings. Cover and cook on low heat for 90 minutes. Remove the bay leaves after 15 minutes; otherwise they will make the *bigos* too bitter.

Soup is the start and glory of any good Polish meal. Polish soups range from a light transparent consommé to a rich creamy broth that can be a meal itself. The most popular soup is *barszcz*, a clear beetroot soup often served with such Polish favorites as sausage, cabbage, potatoes, sour cream, coarse rye bread, and beer.

Poles also enjoy *zurek*, a creamy, sour, white soup with sausage and potato, and *krupnik* (kroop-NEEK), a thick soup made of barley and potato with pieces of bacon and carrots. Soups are often served with *pierogi* (pyer-O-gee), small square pockets of dough filled with a cheesy potato mixture, or mushrooms or cabbage. *Pierogi*, served as dessert, are filled with fruit or jam.

## VODKA AND MORE

For years Poles drank mostly at home, but in cities today, bars have become more popular. Vodka is widely consumed. The Poles claim to have invented the drink, but that claim is hotly disputed by the Russians. Vodka probably originated in the 15th century when there was a fall in the supply of honey, the main ingredient in mead, then the traditional drink. Someone, either Polish or Russian, experimented by distilling alcohol from grain instead, and vodka was created.

Poles drink vodka in small glasses, tossed straight back. There are many varieties of the drink; some are flavored with bison grass, others with juniper or wild cherry. Regardless, the bottle is supposed to be emptied before anyone can leave.

Beer is mostly bottled. There are several regional varieties. The two most popular brands are the strong tasting Tatra Pils and the lighter Piwo Zywiecki.

Many soft drinks are available too, with strawberry and apple being popular flavors. The better fruit juices are made from real fruit, though there are plenty of cheaper, more chemical concoctions available in cartons. Bottled Coca-Cola and Pepsi are available everywhere. Tap water is not always safe for drinking, so Poles buy bottles of mineral water. There is usually one on the table at any meal.

Poland produces several varieties of vodka and beer.

Poles love tea, or *herbata* (herb-A-ta). They drink tea with everything, usually in glasses, without milk and with lemon and a lot of sugar. Polish coffee is a strong brew, reflecting Turkish influence. It is made by pouring water over ground coffee in a glass or cup. Stirring is not advised, unless you want a mouthful of coffee grounds.

*"A guest in the home, God in the home"*

—old Polish proverb

**Wild mushrooms are a delicacy, eaten fresh or dried. These mushrooms are found in the woods in the fall.**

## THE POLISH COOK

The Poles have learned through the centuries to be frugal. Until recently, refrigerators were not found in all homes, particularly in the countryside, so food was dried or preserved. The Poles bottle fruit, pickle cabbage and onions, and dry large wild mushrooms. They search the woods for blueberries, believed to be a remedy for failing eyesight, or blackberries. Children sit along the road, selling berries in jars. In the Tatra foothills, people make goat's milk cheese, which is brown-skinned and looks like a small loaf of bread.

Every home in the village has its own vegetable garden, while an "allotment" on the edge of town serves as a place to grow food crops. In the cities, people check food prices at the supermarket but prefer to buy from a local stall.

In some old countryside homes, food is still cooked on a wood-burning stove topped with an iron plate. The fire below is arranged to provide different cooking temperatures. The center is hottest, for boiling water, and the edges cooler, for simmering soup. The oven section is above the cooking plate and is usually tiled round the sides. This will bake bread, roast meat, and heat the kitchen in winter.

# GOLABKI (CABBAGE ROLLS)

This recipe makes eight to 10 rolls, or four to five servings.

1 cabbage
¼ stick of butter
½ cup minced onions
½ pound (226.8 g) cooked ground beef
¼ teaspoon celery salt

¼ teaspoon Worcester sauce
1 cup cooked rice
1 can tomato soup
½ teaspoon brown sugar

Remove the core of the cabbage. Wash and boil the leafy part for around 10 to 15 minutes, until tender. Rinse in cold water and drain, then separate the leaves. Melt the butter in a pan, and brown the minced onions. Put the ground beef in a large bowl, and add the cooked onions, celery salt, Worchester sauce, and cooked rice, and mix. Lay open the cooked cabbage leaves, one at a time, on a flat plate. Put a small amount of the beef-rice mixture on the leaf. Roll one edge of the leaf up and over the meat, tuck in the sides of the leaf, and continue to roll. Arrange the rolls, seams down, in a greased pan. Mix the tomato soup, water, and brown sugar. Keep a quarter of this mixture, and pour the rest evenly over the rolls. Cover with aluminum foil, and bake at 325°F (162.8°C) for 2 to 2½ hours. Pour some of the reserved sauce mixture over the rolls as they bake to keep them moist. Serve the rolls warm, the more sauce the better.

## *KOLACZKI* (JELLY COOKIES)

This recipe makes two dozen small cookies.

1 pound (453.6 g) cream cheese at room temperature
1 pound (453.6 g) butter at room temperature
6 cups flour
Your favorite flavors of jelly

In a large bowl, mix the cream cheese and butter until a smooth semi-liquid forms. Add the flour, and mix to form a dough. Using a rolling pin, flatten the dough ³⁄₄ inch (1.9 cm) thick on an oiled pan. Using dough cutters, cut out circles, squares, stars, or other shapes from the dough. Make a depression in the center of each piece of dough, and fill with your favorite flavors of jelly. Bake at 375°F (190.6°C) for 10 to 15 minutes, or until lightly browned.

# MAP OF POLAND

Austria, A4, A5, B5

Baltic Sea, A1, B1, C1
Belarus, D1–D3
Beskidy Range, C4
Bialystok, D2
Bielsko-Biala, B4
Biskupin, B2
Bug River, C2, D2–D4
Bydgoszcz, B2

Carpathian Mountains, C4, D4, D5
Chelm, D3
Czech Republic, A3–A5, B4, B5
Czestochowa, B3

Dolnoslaskie, A3, A4, B3, B4

Elblag, C1

Germany, A1–A3
Gdansk, B1
Gdansk Bay, B1, C1
Gdynia, B1
Gliwice, B4
Gniezno, B2

Hungary, B5, C5, D5

Jelenia Gora, A3

Katowice, B4
Kielce, C3
Kolobrzeg, A1
Krakow, C4
Kujawsko-Pomorskie, B2, C2

Lithuania, C1, D1
Lodz, C3
Lodzkie, B2, B3, C2, C3
Lubelskie, C3, D2–D4
Lublin, D3
Lubuskie, A2, A3, B3

Malopolskie, C4
Mazowieckie, C2, C3, D2, D3
Mazurian Lakes, C1, C2

Neisse River, A3

Oder River, A2, A3, B3, B4
Olsztyn, C2
Opolskie, B3, B4
Ostrowiec, C3
Oswiecim, C4

Plock, C2
Podkarpackie, C3, C4, D3, D4
Podlaskie, C2, D1, D2
Pomorskie, B1, B2, C1, C2
Poznan, B2

Radom, C3
Romania, D5
Russia, C1, D1
Rzeszow, D4

Silesia, B3, B4
Slaskie, B3, B4, C3, C4
Slovakia, B4, B5, C4, C5, D4, D5
Sopot, B1
Swietokrzyskie, C3, C4
Szczecin, A2

Torun, B2

Ukraine, D3–D5
Ustka, B1

Vistula River, B1, B2

Walbrzych, B3
Warminsko-Mazurskie, B1, B2, C1, C2, D1, D2
Warsaw, C2
Warta River, A2, B2, B3, C3, C4
Wielkopolskie, A2, A3, B2, B3
Wroclaw, B3

Zachodniopomorskie, A1, A2, B1, B2
Zakopane, C4
Zamosc, D3
Zielona Gora, A3

# ECONOMIC POLAND

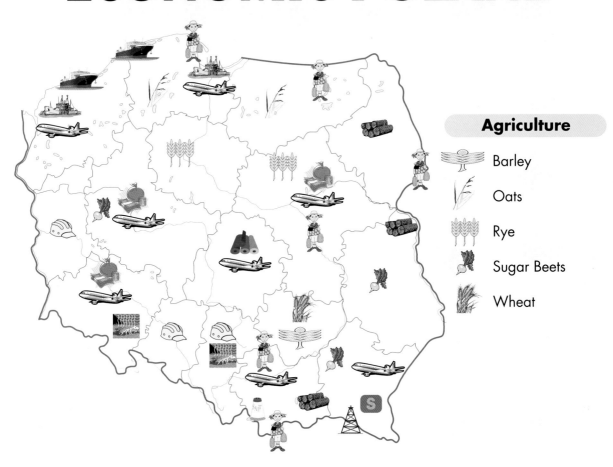

## Agriculture

- Barley
- Oats
- Rye
- Sugar Beets
- Wheat

## Services

- Airport
- Finance
- Port
- Tourism

## Manufacturing

- Forest Products
- Shipbuilding
- Textiles

## Natural Resources

- Coal
- Natural Gas
- Oil
- Salt
- **S** Sulfur

# ABOUT THE ECONOMY

## OVERVIEW

Since 1990 Poland's economy has been changing from central-control communist to capitalist. The high social cost of dealing with unemployment and displacement has slowed the process. Entry to the European Union will add to economic change in Poland. Some of the most dramatic changes are likely to occur in agriculture, as the mechanized, chemical approach of agribusiness replaces traditional, organic farming methods.

## GROSS DOMESTIC PRODUCT (GDP)

US$189 billion (2000 estimate)

## GDP SECTORS

Services 65.9 percent, industry 31 percent, agriculture 3.1 percent (2003 estimate)

## WORK FORCE

18 million (2000 estimate)

## UNEMPLOYMENT RATE

18 percent

## CURRENCY

1 zloty (PLN) = 100 groszy
USD 1 = PLN 4 (2004)
Notes: 10, 20, 50, 100, 200 zloty
Coins: 1, 2, 5 zloty; 1, 2, 5, 10, 20, 50 groszy

## AGRICULTURAL OUTPUT

Grain products, pork, dairy products, potatoes, horticultural products, beets, oilseed products

## INDUSTRIAL OUTPUT

Heavy machinery, iron and steel, raw minerals, ships, automobiles, furniture, textile products, chemicals, processed food, glass

## MAIN EXPORTS

Agricultural and forest products, industrial machinery, chemicals, raw minerals

## MAIN IMPORTS

Crude oil, automobiles, automobile parts, pharmaceutical products, electronic goods

## MAJOR TRADE PARTNERS

Germany, Russia, France, Italy, United Kingdom, Czech Republic, Netherlands

## INTERNATIONAL AIRPORTS

Okecie (Warsaw), TriCity (Gdansk), John Paul II (Krakow)

## PORTS AND HARBORS

Gdansk, Gdynia, Gliwice, Kolobrzeg, Szczecin, Ustka

## INFLATION RATE

0.7 percent (2003 estimate)

## EXTERNAL DEBT

US$64 billion (2002)

# CULTURAL POLAND

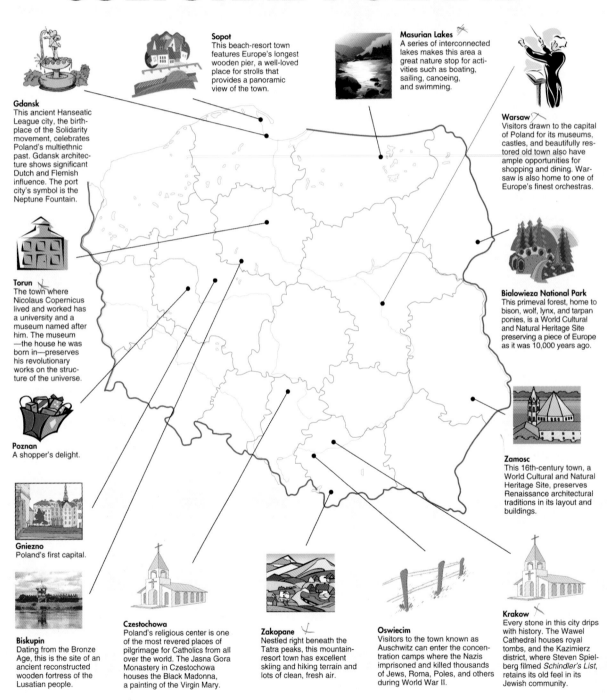

**Sopot**
This beach-resort town features Europe's longest wooden pier, a well-loved place for strolls that provides a panoramic view of the town.

**Masurian Lakes**
A series of interconnected lakes makes this area a great nature stop for activities such as boating, sailing, canoeing, and swimming.

**Warsaw**
Visitors drawn to the capital of Poland for its museums, castles, and beautifully restored old town also have ample opportunities for shopping and dining. Warsaw is also home to one of Europe's finest orchestras.

**Gdansk**
This ancient Hanseatic League city, the birthplace of the Solidarity movement, celebrates Poland's multiethnic past. Gdansk architecture shows significant Dutch and Flemish influence. The port city's symbol is the Neptune Fountain.

**Torun**
The town where Nicolaus Copernicus lived and worked has a university and a museum named after him. The museum —the house he was born in—preserves his revolutionary works on the structure of the universe.

**Bialowieza National Park**
This primeval forest, home to bison, wolf, lynx, and tarpan ponies, is a World Cultural and Natural Heritage Site preserving a piece of Europe as it was 10,000 years ago.

**Poznan**
A shopper's delight.

**Zamosc**
This 16th-century town, a World Cultural and Natural Heritage Site, preserves Renaissance architectural traditions in its layout and buildings.

**Gniezno**
Poland's first capital.

**Biskupin**
Dating from the Bronze Age, this is the site of an ancient reconstructed wooden fortress of the Lusatian people.

**Czestochowa**
Poland's religious center is one of the most revered places of pilgrimage for Catholics from all over the world. The Jasna Gora Monastery in Czestochowa houses the Black Madonna, a painting of the Virgin Mary.

**Zakopane**
Nestled right beneath the Tatra peaks, this mountain-resort town has excellent skiing and hiking terrain and lots of clean, fresh air.

**Oswiecim**
Visitors to the town known as Auschwitz can enter the concentration camps where the Nazis imprisoned and killed thousands of Jews, Roma, Poles, and others during World War II.

**Krakow**
Every stone in this city drips with history. The Wawel Cathedral houses royal tombs, and the Kazimierz district, where Steven Spielberg filmed *Schindler's List*, retains its old feel in its Jewish community.

# ABOUT THE CULTURE

**OFFICIAL NAME**
Rzeczpospolita Polska (Republic of Poland)

**LAND AREA**
117,555 square miles (304,465 square km)

**POPULATION**
38,626,349 (2004 estimate)

**CAPITAL**
Warsaw

**ADMINISTRATIVE DIVISIONS**
Zachodniopomorskie, Pomorskie, Warminsko-Mazurskie, Podlaskie, Mazowieckie, Kujawsko-Pomorskie, Wielkopolskie, Lubuskie, Dolnoslaskie, Opolskie, Lodzkie, Swietokrzyskie, Lubelskie, Podkarpackie, Malopolskie, Slaskie

**NATIONAL FLAG**
White top half, red bottom half

**NATIONAL ANTHEM**
*Mazurek Dabrowskiego* (Dombrowski's Mazurka)

**NATIONAL LANGUAGE**
Polish

**ETHNIC GROUPS**
Polish 96.7 percent, German 0.4 percent, Ukrainian 0.1 percent, Belarusian 0.1 percent, other 2.7 percent (2002)

**MAJOR RELIGION**
Roman Catholicism

**LIFE EXPECTANCY**
Approximately 74 years; men 70 years, women 78.5 years (2004 estimate)

**IMPORTANT HOLIDAYS**
Constitution Day (May 3), National Independence Day (November 11), and all major church festivals

**IMPORTANT POLITICAL LEADERS**
Jozef Pilsudski—first chief-of-state of independent Poland (1918–22)
Wladyslaw Raczkiewicz—president of the Polish government-in-exile (1939–45)
Lech Walesa—Solidarity leader; president of the Republic of Poland (1990–95)
Aleksander Kwasniewski—president of the Republic of Poland (1995–)

**OTHER IMPORTANT FIGURES**
Nicolaus Copernicus (astronomer), Marie Curie (physicist), Karol Jozef Wojtyla (Pope), Stefan Wyszynski (cardinal), Wislawa Szymborska and Adam Mickiewicz (poets), Frederic Chopin and Witold Lutoslawski (composers), Andrzj Wajda (filmmaker), Artur Rubinstein (pianist), Czeslaw Miloscz (writer)

# TIME LINE

| IN POLAND | IN THE WORLD |
|---|---|
| **700s B.C.**<br>Celtic groups arrive. | **753 B.C.**<br>Rome is founded. |
| **500s B.C.**<br>Germanic groups expand from the West. | |
| **A.D. 500s**<br>First Slavic groups arrive. | **116–17 B.C.**<br>The Roman Empire reaches its greatest extent. |
| **A.D. 966**<br>Piast rule begins, Gniezno as capital. | **A.D. 600**<br>Height of Mayan civilization |
| **1038**<br>The capital is moved to Krakow. | **1000**<br>The Chinese perfect gunpowder and<br>begin to use it in warfare. |
| **1370**<br>The Piast dynasty ends. | |
| **1385**<br>The Jagellonian dynasty begins. | |
| **1543**<br>Copernicus's *Concerning the Revolutions of the Celestial Spheres* is published. | **1530**<br>Beginning of trans-Atlantic slave trade organized by the Portuguese in Africa. |
| **1572**<br>The Jagiellonian dynasty ends. | **1558–1603**<br>Reign of Elizabeth I of England |
| **1596**<br>The capital is moved to Warsaw. | **1620**<br>Pilgrims sail the *Mayflower* to America. |
| **1683**<br>Sobieski's army defeats Turks at Vienna. | |
| **1772**<br>First Partition. | |
| **1793**<br>Second Partition. | **1789–99**<br>The French Revolution |
| **1795**<br>Third Partition; last of Polish lands taken | |
| **1830**<br>November uprising against Russia. | |
| **1846, 1848**<br>Krakow and Wielkopolska uprisings. | **1861**<br>The U.S. Civil War begins. |
| **1863–65**<br>January uprising against Russia. | **1914**<br>World War I begins. |
| **1918**<br>A democratic Polish state is created. | **1918**<br>World War I ends. |

| IN POLAND | IN THE WORLD |
|---|---|
| **1919–20** | |
| Polish-Soviet War | |
| **1926** | |
| Marshal Pilsudski's coup | |
| **1939** | **1939** |
| Germany invades Poland. | World War II begins. |
| **1944** | |
| Warsaw uprising. Germans level the city. | **1945** |
| **1947** | The United States drops atomic bombs on |
| Poland becomes a Communist republic. | Hiroshima and Nagasaki. |
| | **1949** |
| | The North Atlantic Treaty Organization |
| | (NATO) is formed. |
| **1956** | |
| Industrial strikes in Poznan | **1957** |
| | The Russians launch Sputnik. |
| | **1966–69** |
| **1970** | The Chinese Cultural Revolution |
| Food riots in Gdansk | |
| **1978** | |
| Karol Wojtyla is elected Pope John Paul II. | |
| **1980** | |
| Solidarity strikes in Gdansk. Czeslaw Milosz | |
| wins the Nobel Prize in literature. | |
| **1981–83** | |
| Martial law | **1986** |
| **1990** | Nuclear power disaster at Chernobyl, Ukraine |
| Lech Walesa is first freely elected president. | **1991** |
| **1995** | Break-up of the Soviet Union |
| Aleksander Kwasniewski becomes president. | |
| **1997** | **1997** |
| A democratic constitution is adopted. | Hong Kong is returned to China. |
| **1999** | |
| Poland joins NATO. | **2001** |
| | Terrorists crash planes in New York, |
| | Washington, D.C., and Pennsylvania. |
| | **2003** |
| **2004** | War in Iraq |
| Poland joins the European Union. | |

# GLOSSARY

**bigos** (BEE-goss)
A favorite Polish dish of sauerkraut, cabbage, mushrooms, onions, and various meats.

**collective farming**
A system in which a number of farms are run as a unit by a community under state supervision.

**communism**
A stage of society, according to Marxist theory, in which all forms of private property are abolished.

**Flying University**
An educational institution founded in Poland in 1882. It did not have a fixed location; instead, classes moved from house to house.

**Gorale** (goor-A-le)
The Polish highlanders of the Tatra Mountains.

**icon**
A holy image that is venerated as sacred.

**Iron Curtain**
The ideological barrier that isolated the Soviet Union and its Communist allies from the West.

**Ł, ł**
A letter in the Polish alphabet that is pronounced like the letter "w" in English.

**Mass**
The service in Roman Catholic churches during which worshipers receive the sacrament of Holy Communion.

**partition**
The division of a country into two or more separate political territories. Poland was partitioned three times in the 18th century, until it completely disappeared as an independent country.

**Podhale** (pod-HA-le)
The meadows in the Tatra foothills where the Gorale live.

**Politburo**
The chief policy-making body of the Communist Party.

**resistance**
An underground organization fighting for the freedom of their nation.

**Russification**
Imperial Russia's policy of replacing the native language and culture in education and business with Russian language and culture.

**Sejm**
Poland's lower house of parliament.

**socialism**
A transitional stage of society, according to Marxist theory, in which the means of production are state-owned and state-controlled.

**Solidarity**
The labor movement that became the political opposition to the Communist regime in Poland through the 1980s.

# FURTHER INFORMATION

**BOOKS**

Andronik, Catherine M. *Copernicus: Founder of Modern Astronomy*. Great Minds of Science series. Hillside, NJ: Enslow Publishing, 2002.

Cipkowski, Peter. *Revolution in Eastern Europe: Understanding the Collapse of Communism in Poland, Hungary, East Germany, Czechoslovakia, Romania and the Soviet Union*. New York, NY: Wiley, 1991.

Craig, Mary. *Lech Walesa: The Leader of Solidarity and Campaigner for Freedom and Human Rights in Poland*. People Who Have Helped the World series. Milwaukee, WI: Gareth Stevens, 1990.

Drucker, Malka and Michael Halperin. *Jacob's Rescue: A Holocaust Story*. New York, NY: Yearling Books, 1994.

Kuniczak, W. S. and Pat Bargielski. *The Glass Mountain: Twenty-Eight Ancient Polish Folktales and Fables*. New York, NY: Hippocrene Books, 1997.

Pasachoff, Naomi. *Marie Curie: And the Science of Radioactivity*. Oxford Portraits in Science series. New York, NY and Oxford, UK: Oxford University Press, 1997.

Popescu, Julian. *Poland*. Major World Nations series. Philadelphia, PA: Chelsea House, 2000.

Uri Orlev. *Run, Boy, Run*. Translated by Hillel Halkin. Boston, MA: Houghton Mifflin/Walter Lorraine Books, 2003.

*Aniela Kaminski's Story: A Voyage from Poland During World War II*. Journey to America series. New York, NY: Berkley Publishing Group, 2001.


**WEBSITES**

BBC News Country Profiles: Poland.
   http://news.bbc.co.uk/1/hi/world/europe/country_profiles/1054681.stm

Central Intelligence Agency World Factbook (select Poland from country list).
   www.cia.gov/cia/publications/factbook

KRYKIET.COM: Online Gateway to Poland. www.krykiet.com

Magical Krakow. www.krakow.pl/en

Ministry of Foreign Affairs of the Republic of Poland. www.msz.gov.pl

Official website of the City of Warsaw. www.e-warsaw.pl

Polish Internet search engine. www.poland.pl

Polska: Poland in Brief (with national anthem audio). www.poland.gov.pl

President of the Republic of Poland. www.prezydent.pl

Sejm of the Republic of Poland (the Polish parliament). www.sejm.gov.pl

Warsaw Voice (Poland's largest English-language weekly newspaper). www.warsawvoice.pl

The World Bank Group (type "Poland" in the search box). www.worldbank.org

# BIBLIOGRAPHY

Bradley, John. *Eastern Europe*. New York, NY: Franklin Watts, 1992.

Donica, Ewa and Sharman, Tim. *We Live in Poland*. Hove, UK: Wayland, 1985.

Horn, Alfred and Pietras, Bozena (editors). *Insight Guides: Poland*. APA Publications, 1992.

Kaye, Tony. *Lech Walesa*. New York, NY: Chelsea House, 1989.

# INDEX